# Three:Sixteens

## Ten Sermons on 3:16 Texts

By

### M. E. Dodd, A.M., D.D., LL.D.

Shreveport, La.

## Wm. B. Eerdmans Publishing Company

Grand Rapids, Michigan

# DEDICATION

This Volume
is gratefully inscribed
to
my children
Dorothy, Helen, Monroe, Martha, Lucile
in appreciation of their loving consideration
of the fact that their father is a
Minister of the Gospel

# FOREWORD

The Bible was first divided into chapters and verses by Cardinal Hugo about 1250.

It is a mere coincidence, of course, but quite remarkable and very impressive to discover that chapters 3 and verses 16 of the various books of the Bible contain such a wealth of spiritual treasures. This is particularly true of the New Testament.

In a ministry approaching a quarter of a century with the same congregation one must be in constant search of attractive, interesting, and helpful means and methods of presenting his message. In pursuing such a quest I fell upon the idea of using the 3:16's of the New Testament for a series of sermons to my own people.

These were stenographically reported and with scant opportunity for revision, correction, and polishing up, they are now given to the publisher in much the same form as public addresses.

I have found these explorations and excavations personally profitable. These findings are sent forth with the hope and prayer that others may find a like spiritual blessing.

# CONTENTS

Matthew 3:16

I N OUR search for the oil fields of God's
grace we have decided to establish a location
in the third chapter of Matthew at verse sixteen. I will read the context:

Matthew 3:13-17, Then cometh Jesus from
Galilee to Jordan unto John, to be baptized of
him. (14) But John forbad him, saying, I have
need to be baptized of thee, and comest thou
to me? (15) And Jesus answering said unto him,
Suffer *it to be so* now; for thus it becometh
us to fulfil all righteousness. Then he suffered
him. (16) And Jesus, when he was baptized,
went up straightway out of the water: and, lo,
the heavens were opened unto him, and he saw
the Spirit of God descending like a dove, and
lighting upon him: (17) And lo, a voice from
heaven, saying, This is my beloved Son, in
whom I am well pleased.

Now strangely enough Luke 3:16 deals with
the same subject so we have two three-sixteens
in one, for this morning.

There are seven Trinities in this Scripture.

There were three representative individuals:
John, the baptizer; Jesus, the subject; and the
crowd looking on as observers and as students.
There were three dramatic acts here; they went
down *into* the water; He was baptized *in* the
water; He came up *out* of the water. There
were three spiritual symbols: the burial and

11

resurrection of our Lord and Saviour Jesus Christ symbolized in the form of the act; the burial of the believer's old life of sin and his resurrection to a new life of righteousness; the expressed faith and hope of the disciple that though his body after the flesh should perish, it should be raised from the dead. There were three Divine persons manifesting themselves here: God the Father; God the Son; and God the Holy Ghost. The three persons of the deity were revealed in a threefold manner; the Son in physical form; the Father's voice; the Holy Spirit descending like a dove. There were three experiences: Christ saw heaven, heard the voice of God, and felt the Spirit descend. There were three examples: an example of obedience; an example of praying; and an example of service. Each of these seven Trinities is exceedingly important and a careful study of them would yield much profit. But we shall have time to devote our thinking to only three.

In these three most important Trinities, and incidentally as the others touch them, we shall see the sublime and significant meaning of this wonderful event in the earthly life of our Lord.

The baptism of Jesus has been such a center of controversy, as to its form, that we have lost much of its spiritual meaning in the heat of our debate. But now that the question of its form has been settled by the consensus of scholarship and by the history of Christianity, it is possible for us to concentrate our thinking upon the baptism of Jesus with the view of discovering the more spiritual content which it was intended to present.

Let us consider:

The threefold manifestation of God;
The threefold experience of Christ; and
The threefold example for us to follow.

Here is a definite, audible, material presentation of the Deity in a Trinity. It is exceedingly important that we get a view of this picture as portrayed by Matthew and Luke.

Throughout the Scriptures the Trinity is revealed. God as a Trinity starts at the very beginning of the Bible. "Let us make man." The pronoun is plural and is found in the very first chapter of Genesis. The Trinity is seen in all the Scriptures.

But the eyes of men were blinded and their hearts were stupefied. They stumbled at the mystery of the Trinity, because of their efforts to objectify God in physical form. They could not think of three persons in one without thinking of them as being separate. And to think of the three as apart from each other would make three Gods. We Christians as Trinitarians are sometimes accused by the Unitarians of having three Gods instead of one. That is not true. It is only three manifestations of the One God represented by God the Father, God the Son and God the Holy Ghost.

There are many illustrations which we might give of the Trinity. I stand before you as a person. You say: "There is a person; it is Dr. Dodd." Well, all right, what do you mean, that

this body which you see with the eyes of flesh
is the person, or that this mind which reasons
and thinks and sometimes stimulates your
thinking is the person or that this heart that
loves every one of you with a deep and death-
less devotion, that this is the person? Yes and
no. Yes because each of these is part of him,
but it takes all three of them to make up the
one person. You cannot conceive of a person
here in a body without a brain or heart. You
can conceive of a person as a spirit without a
brain or a body. Oh, yes you can, because some
of you tell me, "I'll be with you at church in
spirit, but I have to go see grandma next Sunday." I have been preaching to spirits sitting
in empty pews a long time and have never had
a convert among them yet. I had rather see the
body and brain along with the spirit. It takes
the three to make a whole person.

Intelligent people, rational people, sensible
people ought to understand that it is more rea-
sonable to believe in a Trinity than to believe
in Unitarianism. The three are necessary to
make up the one person.

So it is in the God-head — God the Father is
the intelligent nature of Deity, God the Son is
the physical manifestation of Deity, and God
the Holy Ghost is the spiritual revelation of
Deity. These three manifestations or revelations, or projections of Deity into the conscious
life of man compose the whole, the complete
God.

There are those, I know, who emphasize only one person in Deity and therefore they have a one-sided religion. Paul came to Ephesus and found some who had not been baptized into the name of the Trinity, and asked them, "Into what then were you baptized?" and they said, "Into John's baptism, we did not so much as hear whether the Holy Ghost was given."

There are those in our own time who stand on the street corner jumping up and down shouting, "I am filled with the Holy Ghost" and they leave out Jesus the Saviour and God the Father. No, the religion of the Bible, the New Testament, the religion of our Lord and Saviour Jesus Christ is a Trinity religion — God the Father, God the Son and God the Holy Spirit, equal in existence and equal in authority, equal in power, and equal in all matters of the soul of man.

Second, let us consider the threefold experience of Christ.

This threefold experience came through the three primary functions of personality. He saw, He heard, He felt. Those three senses are the ones through which we get ninety-nine per cent of all that we know. He saw the open heaven, He heard the voice of God, He felt the descent of the Holy Ghost. And what do these three experiences mean to him and to us?

Here is what the first one means. He saw heaven opened. He saw. How far can you see? Your physical, natural eyes do not see very far. At sea on a ship you can see the horizon fifteen

miles out. That is why on the plain or on the
ocean you seem to be in the center of a saucer
with a hill rising all around. The higher you
go the further you can see. From an airplane
the higher one goes the further the horizon is
pushed back.

The higher one goes in spiritual experience
the further he can see. The ant can not see very
far. The hog can see a little further. The deer
can see still further. Man ought to be able to
see still further. And God's man ought to be
able to see the furthest of all.

They tell us that the telescope which sweeps
the heavens and makes discoveries of the far
off empires of the universe can see stars millions of light years from the earth. How far
is that? I can't comprehend it. Light travels
at the rate of 186,000 miles a second. Sixty
times that would be what light travels in a minute. Sixty times that would be what light travels in an hour. Twenty-four times that would be
what light travels in a day. And three hundred
and sixty-five times that would be what it travels in a year. That is one light year. One
hundred million times that is the distance to
the furthest outpost of the presently known
universe. If you want to get dizzy, this afternoon, get out your pencil and paper and figure
that out and try to read the figures on the
paper.

But the eye of Jesus went even beyond that.
He could see further than the mightiest telescope has ever peered. In every direction which

man looks in the universe, except in one, he sees
something, a star, a planet, a comet, a sun, a
moon, some object which meets his vision. His
telescope cannot get through and beyond the
material universe. He finds something everywhere he looks except at one spot. Those of you
who have read astronomy lately have been en-
tranced with the study of that open spot in the
north. There is one spot at the north which is
open and clear and no telescope has ever been
able to discover anything in it. It is an opening
in the heavens. The Bible spoke of it thousands
of years ago. It may be fantastic, but I heard
a great Bible teacher last summer at the great
Winona Lake Bible Conference say that this
is the route through which Jesus is coming
when he comes back to this earth. He has a
straight way, a highway, an open way for the
king without stars or planets or anything in
that way.

Now, I think when Jesus saw the open heaven
as His holy eyes opened at His baptism that
He was looking beyond all that man's eye has
or ever will see, looking to the furthermost
reaches of the universe of God, however far
that is, and was seeing heaven, even the heaven
of heavens. He saw God the Father, He saw
the angels, He saw the saints of God, the prophets of God, the redeemed of God — those of
ages past and those of ages to come. Yes, I
think God lifted the curtain and let Him see all
of those who should ever believe on His name
and who should ever be redeemed by His death

on the cross and who should live by the power
of His resurrection. Yes, He saw you and He
saw me in heaven. Isn't it wonderful? Wonderful that He looked down the centuries and
across the ages and through the universe and
saw all the redeemed hosts of God that ever had
been or ever would be given to Him by God the
Father for what He was doing for the world
to the glory of the Father.

Now what does this mean? This means that
men and women live, not by bread alone, but
they live by spiritual vision. That is one thing
which we need to learn, in this materialistic age
of ours, above everything else in this world.
Ninety-nine per cent of our conscious time is
devoted to material things. I sympathize with
doctors especially who have to battle to main-
tain spiritual life because they are constantly
forced to deal with the material things. When
they do win a victory as some of our beloved
doctors have done and become spiritually mind-
ed, God honoring and God serving men, they
deserve more credit than the most of us do.

The Bible says that where there is no vision
the people perish. The world is perishing today, going around in circles, crowding each
other's heels because there is no vision. Personally, classically, nationally, internationally,
all peoples are grasping for material things
and perishing at the same time for the lack of
spiritual vision. "Where there is no vision the
people perish." Spiritual vision is the might-

iest factor and the most dynamic force in the life of men and of women.

The second thing at Jesus' baptism: He heard a voice from heaven. Others did not hear that voice. They probably were like some of you. You say, "No, I don't believe this, that and the other in religion." You ought to follow the wisdom and instruction of the old Negro who said: "You should say I don't believe it not as I knows of." There were those who said, "Why, He is talking out of His head." Why should you, if your radio is not tuned in on KWKH on Sunday evening at 9:00 o'clock, say, "No, there is no radio service from the First Baptist Church?" Your neighbor next door is tuned in on it and gets the service.

Science, instead of confuting the Scriptures, is confirming them. The radio confirms our faith in spiritual reality. The heart that is tuned to the infinite radio of heaven by the finger of God may hear and see what others cannot see and hear.

I heard a radio program from Jerusalem the other night and I said to my family as we sat in the quiet of our room, "Why should it be thought a thing incredible, as we read in the Bible, that when Jesus comes He will stand on Mount Zion and speak to the whole world. And when television has been completed, we in America, we may see one standing in Jerusalem. The Bible says, that when Jesus comes, "every eye shall see Him." Yes, I'll sit in my room or stand in my pulpit and through the vision of spiritual revelation I'll see Him as He is and upon looking at Him I shall be transformed into His likeness, and shall be like Him when He comes. That is what spiritual vision does and what the spirit voice says.

Others couldn't hear, but Jesus did and the voice said, "This is my beloved Son." Here is the fulfillment of all prophecy, and the realization of all the hope of Israel and of the burning hearts of humanity.

Wise men and leaders had long looked for this and had found it not. But when the index finger of God pointed upon Him and the voice from heaven said, "This is He," all voices of the past were focussed there and the music and the ageless poetry united in declaring, "This is He for whom all the nations have sought."

You think of Him as emerging out of that beautiful little city of Nazareth in the hills of Galilee. One of the most beautiful scenes Mrs. Dodd and I saw was when we sat far into the night out on the hillside above Nazareth with the full moon falling upon the white houses and meditated upon the meaning of that matchless, marvelous event. There lay the beautiful little village of His childhood and youth, so quiet, so peaceful, so lovely in the moonlight. But the time came when He could no longer remain there in quiet, perfect seclusion. So emerging out of that beautiful village He comes walking down the Jordan valley to John the Baptist to the Jordan River and offers Himself for baptism. God says, "That is my Son." This is the

Messiah, the King of Israel, this is the Lord of life, the ruler of the world. Afterward that same voice was to say, ''Hear ye him.''

Baptism was the public assumption of His public ministry. The descent of the Holy Ghost upon Him was as if it were the announcement of the coronation of the king.

Last week the whole world was saddened at the death of George V of England. And the world was thrilled with the daring, adventurous spirit of the Prince of Wales who took off in an airplane and flew to London to assume the high office of King of England and to begin his reign over the British Empire with its five hundred millions of people, one-fourth the population of the world. That was his assumption of the throne. The coronation will come later in a formal ceremony for that purpose.

The baptism of Jesus was the announcement and His assumption to the royal throne. The cross was His coronation day. This announcement of Jesus as the Son of God was no new revelation. This was no new discovery to Jesus. It may have been a deepening of His own conviction but it was confirmation of that which He already knew. He knew before His birth and at His birth and at twelve years of age in the Temple and throughout the whole of His earthly pilgrimage that He was the Son of God.

Cerinthus of the first century proclaimed the heresy that Jesus never became the Son of God and never knew that He was the Son of God until His baptism. And through the centuries others have repeated that false doctrine. I heard one of them through my car radio, as I was coming to the church this morning, a teacher of a large Bible Class, say that Jesus Christ never knew He was God's Son until His baptism. That is the heresy of the Cerinthian gnostics of the first century, whom John and Peter and Paul answered in their epistles. Everybody should know better than that now. But if one is foolish enough to try to perpetuate that long worn out heresy then he ought to be answered. Jesus did know from the beginning that He was the Son of God and King of Israel. Was it not announced to the virgin before His conception? Was it not announced at His birth by an angel choir from Heaven? Did He not say at the age of twelve answering and asking questions of the doctors in the temple, "Know ye not that I must be about my Father's business?" He knew it all the time, for He was the Son of God from all eternity.

Dr. A. T. Robertson, the world's greatest Greek Scholar, says in his word pictures in the New Testament, "We are not to understand that this was the beginning of the incarnation of Christ as the Cerinthian gnostics held. But this fresh influx of the Holy Spirit may have deepened the Messianic consciousness of Jesus and certainly revealed Him to the Baptist as God's Son."

Alexander Maclaren said, "It is but the official and solemn announcement of a previous

fact.'' Again: ''I believe that when Christ rose
from the water of baptism that no new gift was
His, but a confirming of that which He knew
from all time.''

We could quote many great scholars and high
authorities to the same effect. I believe that
Jesus was the Son of God from all eternity and
that He knew it from the beginning.

His third experience was that He felt the
descent of the Holy Spirit upon Him. Mark
says; ''the Spirit'', Matthew says; ''The Spirit
of God.'' Luke says; ''The Holy Spirit.'' Now
there is no need to dwell upon the visible form
which the Holy Spirit took. The Bible says,
''like a dove.'' Throughout the Scriptures the
dove is a symbol of purity, of peace, and of
power. And the dove was accepted for a sacrificial offering in the temple. For that reason,
perhaps, it was chosen to represent the Holy
Ghost coming upon Jesus. It was also a fit
representation of His peace and purity and
power. The Holy Spirit, like a dove, brooded
over the chaotic universe and brought order
and system and law out of the confusion into
which the devil had thrown it. This same dove
of peace now came upon Jesus to make Him
the Prince of Peace that the disturbed minds
and torn spirit of humanity might find order
and peace through Him.

Being sinless, Jesus Himself needed no baptism of repentance. But He came to fulfill all
righteousness that He might receive the confirmation of faith from the Father's voice and

the descending Spirit from whom He was to receive all necessary power for the performance of His miracles and mercies.

He healed the sick, opened the eyes of the blind, cast out devils and brought the dead back to life again by the power of the Holy Ghost. The jealous, wicked enemies said, "He is doing this by the power of Beelzebub, the prince of devils." Jesus said to them, "Look out there, that is blasphemy. You are ascribing to the devil the work of the Holy Ghost." That is the unpardonable sin for which there is no forgiveness in this world nor in the world to come.

Finally, here are three great examples:

First, an example of obedience. "It becomes us to fulfill all righteousness." Jesus was baptized, not in order to be made the Son of God, He was already that. He was baptized, not in order to wash away His sin, He had none. He was baptized as a public testimony to be declared the Son of God and in fulfillment of God's will. There was a book known as the gospel of the Hebrews from which Jerome quotes the Lord's mother and brothers as saying: "John the Baptist is baptizing unto the baptism of repentance; let us go and be baptized by Him." But Jesus said unto them, "What sin have I done that I should go and be baptized by John, unless perchance this very thing that I have said is itself an offense?"

The second practical example is that of "praying." This is the first recorded instance of the public prayer life of our Lord. I got out

my own book, "The Prayer Life of Jesus," last
night, for the first time in many years, and read
the chapter on this verse in Luke. You will
find a full discussion of this subject in that volume. "Jesus also being baptized and praying."
"And praying," has a vital relationship to baptism. Baptism is a plain duty for every Christian. Prayer is the privilege of every Christian. What is the relationship of these two?
Here is something for you to think about.

There is no record of Jesus having prayed
prior to His baptism. There is no record of His
having prayed after His resurrection. His baptism opened His public ministry. His burial
closed His public ministry. He prayed only,
between these two events. What are we to
understand from that? For one thing this may
help us to solve the problem of our unanswered
prayers. Of one thing we are sure: that accept-
able and effective prayer is impossible until we
have obeyed the will of God. Is there any
known duty in your life unperformed? Is there
rebellion in your heart and mind against the
thing that God wants you to do? You can't
pray until those things are straightened out.
Obey first and then pray. Don't you say to your
child in the home, "Have you done what I told
you? Well, why ask me for anything until you
have done what I told you?" Why should we
expect God to give us His blessings when we
are living in known disobedience to Him. Jesus

obeyed by being baptized and then He could pray and He never prayed prior to that. He did not need to pray after the thing that baptism prefigured had been fulfilled, namely His resurrection. This is in harmony with the general tenor of the Scriptures.

We read in the First Epistle of John, "Whatsoever we ask of Him, we receive, because we keep His commandments and do those things that are well pleasing in His sight."

And finally: third, of the practical examples is that of service. Jesus went straightway from His baptism to service. From being empowered by the Holy Ghost, and praying, He went straightway to His life of duty and service. No longer could He be hid in His Nazareth home, no longer could He rest. From now on, it was out into the world, out to the battle field, to the conflict and to death on the cross.

The crown that will be placed on the head of Edward VIII at his coronation day has these words on it, "Ich Dien." "I serve." It is a crown of glory to the ruler of the British Empire. Jesus' crown of glory as the son of God, the Lord of life, and King of the world is, "He came not to be ministered unto but to minister."

By faith in Jesus Christ we are children of God and as such are kings and priests unto our God. As such our greatest crown of glory should be that we live — "Not to be ministered unto but to minister and to give our life a ransom for the people.'' Service should be the object and the end of all God's blessings and of all spiritual experience and of all personal powers.

Baptism — the opened heaven — the Father's approving voice — the descent of the Spirit — obedience to God — prayer — service to man — these belong together.

John 3:16

## John 3:16

THE greatest one of all the 3:16's of the Bible is John 3:16. I ask you to come with me, this morning, for an old year meditation on John 3:16:

"God so loved the world, that He gave His only begotten Son, that whosoever believeth in Him should not perish, but have everlasting life."

Every word of that verse shines like a star and glitters like a gem. "GOD," the omnipotent, the eternal, the infinite, the omniscient, the omnipresent, God.

"GOD SO LOVED" — did not hate. It does not say, "I believe in you." He does. It does not say, "I trust you." He does. It does not say, "I provide for you." He does. It does not say, "I will care for you." "God so loved." Love includes everything else.

"GOD SO LOVED THE WORLD" — the whole world, with every sinning, suffering, sorrowing broken piece of humanity in it. He loved all races, colors, and nations.

"GOD SO LOVED THE WORLD THAT HE GAVE" — Love always gives. "That He GAVE." He did not send. He did not offer. He did not order. He did not command. He did not ask. He did not request. "HE GAVE."

"God so loved the world that He gave HIS ONLY BEGOTTEN SON" — He gave His best, biggest, finest possession, even all that He had. It does not say He gave money. That is

31

the last, least, easiest thing anybody can give. He gave life, His own life, even that of His only Son.

"God so loved the world that He gave His only begotten Son, THAT WHOSOEVER BELIEVETH IN HIM." Not whosoever obeys Him, or loves Him, or serves Him, but whosoever believeth. Not whosoever joins the church, or is baptized or takes the Lord's Supper, or anything else, but just whosoever believeth.

"God so loved the world that He gave His only begotten Son, that whosoever believeth in Him SHOULD NOT PERISH." Not, should not hunger, get tired, suffer, be tempted, but should not perish. That looks to the ultimate outcome. Many things may happen to the believer, but the final end is guaranteed, he shall not perish.

"God so loved the world that He gave His only begotten Son, that whosoever believeth in Him should not perish BUT HAVE EVERLASTING LIFE." Oh! How wonderful. Everlasting life, here and now, a present possession, not a promised prospect.

This is the greatest verse, from the greatest book, out of the greatest volume, on the greatest subject, by the greatest author, for the greatest purpose in all the universe of God.

There it is, the good news, the evangel, the gospel, all compact into one verse, through the most thrilling, the most vital sentence ever uttered.

John 3:16 is a little Bible within itself. It

is the essence of all the Bible message. It is the quintessence of all divine revelation.

Alexander Maclaren speaks of it as having four aspects. It is a lake, a great mountain lake, surpassing in beauty Lake Katrine in Scotland or Lake Geneva in Switzerland or any of the other far famed lakes of the world. It is a river flowing in crystal clearness from that lake for the refreshing and saving of the whole world. It is a pitcher with which men may dip into the water for health giving draughts. It is the water of life itself. The lake is the heart of God. His love is the river that brings salvation. "Whosoever believeth" is the pitcher. "Shall have everlasting life" is the draught.

And, then, again, we have here an exposition of divine love. Its origin, in the heart of God. Its extent, to all the world. Its power, so strong that He gave His only begotten Son. Its freeness, that whosoever believeth. And, its effectiveness, should not perish but have everlasting life.

What is the sweetest word you ever heard? What is the most thrilling thing that was ever said to you? Was it not to have grandbaby climb upon your knee at Christmas time and say, " 'Andaddy, I love you;" or to have the children come home at the holiday season and say, "Daddy, Mother, I love you;" or to have father or mother say, "I love you, my child;" or to have husband or wife say, "I love you?" Do not expressions like these give the greatest thrill of anything in the world? Then, does it mean nothing to you to have God say, "I love you." Should not this be to us the most inspiring, the most thrilling, the most satisfying thing said to a human heart?

"God so loved the world that He gave His only begotten Son, that whosoever believeth in Him should not perish but have everlasting life."

You and I do not feel such a thrill over it, because we take it for granted. All our life we have been surrounded with so much of God's love and all He has done for us, that we accept it as a matter of fact. Oh, if we could see the darkness, the travail, the tragedy, the loneliness, and the sorrow out of which people come when it dawns upon them for the first time that God loves them, it would mean so much more to us than it does now. The only God the heathen know is a god of hatred and vengeance. A God of love is something new.

There are many kinds of love. The biologists tell us of physical love, the physical attraction which one has for another in that way. This is the lowest form of love. It can scarcely be called love. It may be mere passion. The psychologist tells us of intellectual love. It is the experience in which one finds intellectual fellowship with another. It is a tie that binds minds together. It is a common thought interest and unity.

Then there is spiritual love between two human beings. It is two hearts beating as one. It is the blending of one spirit into another.

But we have not yet reached the highest manifestation of love. We must climb one more peak. On that topmost summit we find divine love.

Divine love is the highest and the holiest and the purest and the sweetest and the finest of all love. No man, no woman, really knows what love is who has not experienced divine love. Until divine love has been planted in the heart one cannot love fully.

What is divine love that makes it so different from all other love? Why, divine love is the very attribute of God himself. We *have* love. God *is* love.

There are various ways and means by which we may see the attributes of God, His power, knowledge, wisdom, holiness, justice, truth, etc.

We see the power of God in nature. The thunder, the lightnings, the troubled tides of the seas tell us, "There is power, the power of God." Yes, that is God's power manifesting itself. Then we read the law of God in the Old Testament and say, "There is a wisdom, the wisdom of God." Now God demonstrates power and God manifests wisdom. But God is love. Love is the very essence of His being. Love is a quality of His personality. Love is a part of His divine nature. For one to have divine love is to have God. And the more we have of God the more we have of love, and the less we have of God the less we have of love. Now what is this divine love, the love of God that is different from others and that makes our love different when we have it. Here is the standard by which we may test our religious profession and see whether or not it is genuine.

By this we may measure both the quantity and the quality of our professed religion. How far does my love express itself for unlovely people, for the poor, the dirty, the ignorant?

"God so loved the world," the whole of it, including every undeserving person in it. Go with me down the streets of Damascus and see one of those miserable pieces of humanity that is being taken apart by the disease of leprosy. They are loathsome, repulsive, filthy. The first joints of the fingers have come off from some, then the fingers themselves, then the wrist has sloughed off; eyeballs are gone and the sockets are open spaces; the nose is gone from some; the legs are gone. These poor, miserable, filthy, repulsive pieces of humanity lie there in the dirt scarcely able to utter a word, mere stumps of what was a human body. And yet, God loved them and gave His Son, His only begotten Son, to die for them. That is divine love. Can you love like that?

Oh, it is easy enough to love lovely people, charming people, educated people, cultured people. It is natural and human to love our own family, but to love, as God loved, is another thing. Yes, to love physical and moral lepers, not just to be interested in them, not simply to patronize and toss out a coin, but really to love them, that is divine, that is religion.

To love the unlovely and to be able to say, honestly and sincerely, "I love you, I really love you," is indeed divine love. To love people who are utterly opposite from ourselves in every respect — nationally, racially, morally,

socially, educationally, religiously — to love
the naturally disliked people is divine love.

Do certain types of people irritate you? Perhaps you do not like the Negro, you do not like
the Japanese, the Chinese, the German, the
Jew, the Mexican, the Italian. You speak of
them as "Greaser," "Gringo," "Dago,"
"Shenie," "Wop" and what not. You say
"Jap" instead of Japanese, you say "China-
man" instead of Chinese. You do not like them
and you use whatever name of contempt you
have at your command. Well, here is a test of
whether or not divine love is in your heart.
"God so loved the world," all races, all classes,
all kinds, all colors, all religions, all nations.
He loved them. That is a pretty severe test, is
it not? We, too, must love them if we are to
be Godlike.

I am afraid at times that we haven't very
much religion, that we do not love as we should.

And then God loves His enemies, and that
is a test of our love. God commends His love
to us in that while we were yet sinners, He
gave His Son to die for us. While we were taking the holy name of God in vain, when we were
enemies against God, fighting God, God's
church, God's minister, God's work, He loved
us. He loved us when we were His enemies.
He loves the bitterest enemy in all the world.

Do you have an enemy who would do you
harm? Do you have an enemy who would destroy your home, your business, who would
steal your money, burn your house, kidnap your
baby, do anything in the world against you?

Can you love him? God did. God does. And that is the test of whether our love is divine love.

In *Quo Vadis,* the great Polish author makes one of his characters say: "The Greeks gave us learning, the Romans gave us law, what has Christianity given us?" Another character answers, "Love." That is what Christ has given to the world — Love.

As Kagawa says, "No man can know the love of God until he has found the revelation of God in Jesus Christ."

What is the extent of God's love? The whole world, all kinds and classes and individuals, which includes me. The miracle of miracles and marvel of marvels, the one which surpasses all other miracles, is that God should love me. Knowing myself as I do and despising myself as I do for the mean and despicable things that are inside me, I marvel beyond words that God should love me. I have no difficulty in believing other miracles when I see this one.

And then the power of that love is that it "gave." It gives the best, not that which is left over, nor that which is of no use, but its best. Love always gives. God gave His only begotten Son to the world in order that He might also give the world to His Son.

Let us note, then, the freeness of that love —whosoever believeth on Christ. If you leave out Christ, you leave out the heart of the whole matter. It is not simply belief in God, but belief on Christ. No man can be saved apart from Christ.

Then, too, we see the effectiveness of that love. It produces eternal life for those who believe in Christ. Love and life constitute the theme song of God's gospel. Forty-three times in this gospel John speaks of eternal life. Those who have everlasting life shall never perish, shall never be dissolved, shall never be pulled apart.

Going back to the Greek we see something new here. It is this: He that receives God through Christ shall have everlasting life, that is never-aging life, shall have perpetual youth. John 3:16 is the long fabled fountain of youth.

The other day I saw a health chart. It showed that physical life reaches its maximum at twenty-five years of age. Think of the athletes who are out at thirty. One reaches at twenty-five the maximum physical power. But the chart shows that intellectual life may go on climbing to one hundred without reaching its apex. The chart's black line showed physical life climbing to its climax at twenty-five and then beginning to descend. The blue line showed intellectual life climbing to one hundred. Now, there might have been a crimson line on the chart representing the spiritual life of one who accepts Christ. It would have climbed higher and even higher, going on indefinitely, never-ending, enjoying eternal never-aging life.

"You are looking older." "What mean these gray hairs?" "What meaneth that tottering form?" "What meaneth the toothless mouth?" "What mean these dim eyes?" Whether we like it or not, it means we are getting older and

that this old form is going to the grave some
day. Such is this life in this world. But there
is a world of perpetual youth, of everlasting
youth, eternal youth in God through Christ.

No wonder Kagawa sang in his beautiful
poems from the slums:

*My God is Love;*
*My God is Love,*
*Tender and deep;*
*I feel His close, sweet presence*
*Looking down to see*
*The beggar-baby*
*Lying in my arms asleep.*

And then he cries out as he looks out upon
the world: "Ah, this famine of love! How it
saddens my soul in city and country, in hospi-
tal and factory, in shop and on street, ever this
dreadful drought of love! Not a drop of love
anywhere; the loveless land is more dreary than
Sahara and more terrible than Gobi. When the
last drop of love has dried away all men will
go mad and begin to massacre all who ever
thought of love or appreciated it."

*"I know not where His islands lift*
*Their fronded palms in air,*
*I only know I cannot drift*
*Beyond His love and care."*

As the old year passes, as the days go flit-
ting by, and we come ever nearer to the end of
the journey, the thought of God's love casts
out all fear. It casts out all anxiety; it casts
out all sorrow. God loves me and that is enough.
I am satisfied. Amen!

Acts 3:16

## Acts 3:16

AND His name through faith in His name hath made this man strong, whom ye see and know: yea, the faith which is by Him hath given him this perfect soundness in the presence of you all.''

What is your name? How much weight does your name carry in the circle in which you move? How far and wide has your name gone? What does your family name stand for in the community where you live?

Dean Brown asks this question as a chapter heading in one of his brilliant books. By the question he does not mean what are the letters that spell out your name, but he means, what do people think of when they hear your name called? What does your name stand for? When we hear one name called, it may stand for all that is good, while another name stands for all that is bad.

Suppose I call a list of names and you test it in your own thinking. What is the reaction in your mind when I call the name of Moses? Is it not law? David? That is music, poetry, the Psalms. Socrates and Plato? Philosophy. Demosthenes? That is oratory. Shakespeare? Literature. Napoleon? That is war and fighting. Spurgeon? That is preaching.

What do you think of when you hear these
names called? What do people think of when
they hear your name called? The word I pro-
nounced, what you heard from my voice was
not the names of these people, but what they
stand for in your thinking is their names.

Now when you hear the name of God, what
do you think of? The Bible uses many words
or titles in its effort to convey the name of God,
in the sense of interpreting His character and
work. What are some of these names?

One's name may stand for many things. A
man may be an artist, a literary genius, a public speaker, a teacher, a scientist, explorer, a
traveler, all in one. You may think of several
things when you hear certain names, so varied
are their personalities, and character and conduct and service to the world. This is pre-em-
inently true of God. His character and work are
so multiplied that many names are required.

In Genesis God asked the question of one,
"What is thy name?" And then the same question was asked of God, "What is thy name?"

"This is my name forever," said the Lord
God. And, "Thy name is great," said Jeremiah. Jehovah is that name: He that is, He
that was and He that is to be.

Campbell Morgan says, "The name of God
stands for the Great 'I am, I was, and I shall
be.' "

The other name which represents the character and personality of Deity, the Eternal,

Self Existent One is Elohime. It is a name that stands for strength, faithfulness and loyalty.

Besides this primary fundamental name of God, there are seven other words which express the Work of God.

1. Jehovah Jireh, Gen. 22:8, "The Lord will provide."

2. Jehovah Rapha, Ex: 15:26, "The Lord that Healeth."

3. Jehovah Nissi, Ex. 17:15, "The Lord our Banner."

4. Jehovah Shalom, Judges 6:24, "The Lord our peace."

5. Jehovah Raah, Ps. 23, "The Lord my shepherd."

6. Jehovah Tsedkinu, Jer. 23:6, "The Lord our righteousness."

7. Jehovah Shammah, Ezek. 48:35, "The Lord is ever present."

What are your personal needs? Whatever they are the name of God is sufficient for them and can supply every need. If that need be comfort, righteousness, salvation, preservation, provision, whatever it is the name of God stands for that and God is that, and God can do that.

Now the name by which the apostle healed that sick man was the name of God, the name of Jesus, the name of the Lord, the name of Christ: our Lord Jesus Christ is His full name.

There are 312 titles or names ascribed to our Lord Jesus Christ throughout the Bible. Jesus is His human name, by which He saves His people from their sin. Christ, the anointed One, is His heavenly name. His name is Immanuel, God with us. His character and personality are so multiplied and His work so varied that it required a great number of titles and designations by which He might be made known to the human mind.

And whatever interest or need one may have Jesus has a name to fit that need. To the artist, He is the one altogether lovely. To the astronomer, He is the Sun of Righteousness, the Bright and Morning Star. To the baker, He is the Living Bread. To the biologist, He is the Life. To the builder, He is the sure Foundation. To the carpenter, He is the Door. To the doctor, He is the Great Physician. To the educator, He is the Great Teacher. To the farmer, He is the Sower and the Lord of the Harvest. To the florist, He is the Rose of Sharon and the Lily of the Valley. To the geologist, He is the Rock of Ages. To the horticulturist, He is the True Vine. To the judge, He is the Righteous Judge, the Judge of all men. To the juror, He is the faithful and True Witness. To the lawyer, He is the Counsellor, the Lawgiver, the Advocate. To the newspaper man, He is the Good Tidings of Great Joy. To the oculist, He is the Light of the Eyes. To the philanthropist, He is the Unspeakable Gift. To the preacher, He is the Word of God. To the railroad man, He is the New and Living Way. To the sculptor, He is the Living Stone. To the statesman, He is the Desire of all Nations. To the student, He is the Incarnate Truth. To the theologian, He is the Author and Finisher of our Faith. To the toiler, He is the Giver of Rest. To the sinner, He is the Lamb of God, which taketh away the sin of the world. To the Christian, He is the Son of the Living God, the Saviour, the Redeemer and Lord.

WHAT IS CHRIST TO YOU? When His name is mentioned what does it signify to your mind and to your heart?

It was by His name that devils were cast out; by His name that the sick were healed; by His name that the devils were made obedient; by His name the dead were raised; and by His name sins were forgiven. And if there is any other human need His name will supply it. By His name the apostles and disciples conquered.

In the name of Jesus we are to be baptized; in the name of Jesus we are to assemble for worship, with the promise of His presence; in the name of Jesus, Christians are to render all service even to giving a cup of cold water; in the name of Jesus we are to suffer; in His Name we are to pray, with the assurance that "whatsoever ye ask in My name, that will I do that the Father may be glorified in the Son."

> "Take the name of Jesus with you
> Child of sorrow and of woe;
> It will joy and comfort give you,
> Take that name where'er you go."

> "How sweet the name of Jesus sounds
> In a believer's ears,
> It soothes his sorrows, heals his wounds
> And drives away his fears."

Finally: We are to be accepted in heaven by
God the Father in the name of Jesus our Saviour. In that name, through faith we have received cleansing from sin and sonship in His
family and are therefore accepted before the
Father by the name of Jesus. "By His name,
through faith in His name this man hath been
made whole."

We are justified by faith, we are saved by
faith, we are overcomers of the world by faith,
we are to pray in faith, work in faith, and accomplish God's glory, by faith.

The only thing by which we can limit the
power of God is our lack of faith. You and I
must have that faith if we are to do work for
Him.

My observation of Christianity in America
and around the world, convinces me that our
great sin is that we lack faith, dynamic, glor-
ious faith in God. We are looking to all sorts
of human ingenuity, schemes and plans rather
than to the name of Christ and the power of
God. We are limiting the power of God by our
unbelief. We do not believe in our Bible, nor
in the Holy Ghost, nor in Christ Jesus, nor in
God Almighty.

A very intelligent and scholarly man used to
go every chance he had to hear Billy Sunday.
He was asked "Why do you go to hear him?
You don't believe what he says." "No, but he
does." And when the church of Jesus Christ
believes what it professes, the flood tides of

God's Holy Ghost will come on the earth and
all our affairs will be disposed of by the wisdom
and power of God.

What is the use of having electric fixtures in
the building if the lights are not connected?
What is the use of having water fixtures in the
building if the water pipe is cut off?

I remember a few years ago when we had a
water shortage in Shreveport. It was not because there was not sufficient water out there
in the Cross Lake reservoir, but because the
carrying channel was not sufficient to bring it
here. God's reservoir is not exhausted. God's
reservoir is as full as ever. Our only difficulty
is our carrying channel of faith has been
choked up and God's power cannot flow
through.

I read in the papers the stories of our great
new Rodesa oil field. They have brought in a
great gusher capable of producing forty thousand barrels of oil a day. But it has been
choked down to 150 barrels a day. Here are
God's gushers, His oil wells of grace, ready to
pour their healing streams of mercy upon all
humanity if only given a channel through which
to flow. Unbelief has choked it off.

The Apostles had faith in the healing power
of that name. They urged the impotent man
to have faith. This combined faith won the day.

Peter reached down his right hand and lifted
him up. He was a "Right Handed Christian."
The man felt something surging through his
body that he had never felt before. He tried his

limbs and body and heart and found them sound. The first thing he did was to exclaim, "Glory to God in the highest." Peter said to the people, "Why look on us, as though we were anything?" "Give God the glory."

Don't look upon us, we are only men. But through faith in the name of the Christ of God and the God of the Christ is this thing done. It was a demonstration of the power of God, not of men.

The question is this: When the people of the world look upon you and me do they give glory to God because they have discovered in us a manifestation of the name and power of God in this world? Are your business contacts and your social life; your political voting and all the rest, such as to commend the name of Jesus to a lost world that needs its saving, healing power?

How sweet to the Christian! Here is the name of Jesus, the name above every name in Heaven above, in earth below or in the things beneath the earth, the name that is above every name.

1 Corinthians 3:16

## 1 Corinthians 3:16

IN OUR quest for spiritual light in the three-sixteens of the New Testament we come now to I Cor. 3:16, for tonight: "Know ye not that ye are the temple of God, and that the Spirit of God dwelleth in you?"

The Weymouth translation says this, "You are God's sanctuary and the spirit of God has His home within you."

There are two words in the Greek which refer to the temple of worship. The word used here refers to the inner temple, the sacred place, the place of God's dwelling. You are the place of God's residence in the world.

A little child climbs on your knee and says, "Daddy, where does God live?" And, usually, you go pointing off yonder somewhere. If you were wise and more accurate you would say very modestly and humbly, "Why baby, God lives right here in my heart." This is His place of residence in the world. Ye are God's temple, ye are the sanctuary in which God lives in the world.

My family and I were going down 16th street in Washington, D. C., for our service on Sunday morning in the National Memorial Baptist Church. Just before we arrived at Columbia Road we noticed a beautiful church house, not the one we were seeking, but one which attracted our attention. On a beautiful bulletin board we read these words, "Wherever my head has a pillow, God shall have a house." I paused long enough to call that to the attention of our children, wishing them to remember always that wherever their head finds a resting place there God's spirit may find a home.

We read in the New Testament about the evil spirits that were cast out of wicked men and they went to and fro in the earth seeking a place of rest and finding none. Then they came back to that self same human heart and finding nobody else occupying it they entered in again and the second state of that man was worse than the first. If the swept and garnished house of this man had only given hospitality to the Spirit of God, how different would have been his life!

I wonder if the Spirit of God does not go to and fro in the earth seeking a dwelling place, and wishing us to have the attitude of mind and heart that wherever our head finds a resting place, "God's Spirit shall find a home."

There are many temples throughout the world of various sorts. But the most divine and most sacred temple in all the world is the temple of the human body in which the Spirit of God dwells. This ties on very closely to what I was saying this morning from Colossians 3:16 about the word of God dwelling in you richly. "Know ye not that ye are the temple of God" and that being His sanctuary He dwells in you.

Of course to a Christian the great interest he finds in visiting various parts of the world is in seeing the great temples of worship. There is Westminster Abbey, where the great of the British Empire are buried. And there is St. Paul's in London which is the center of religious interest for the Episcopalian people of all the world.

Then we go down into the city of Rome and visit St. Peter's, which is the central temple for the Roman Catholics of all the world. The tesselated floors, the marble columns, the marvelous stained glass windows, the golden altar, the gorgeous tapestries, the massive dome, all make a most wonderful temple.

We might go on visiting other great and historic temples of worship throughout the Christian world. In France we visit the Rheims Cathedral, where Joan of Arc crowned the Dauphin and which was so barbarously shelled by the Germans during the World War. In Milan we visit the church house on whose walls Da Vinci painted his masterpiece, "The Last Supper," and in which Napoleon afterwards stabled his horses. In Venice there is St. Mark's, so exquisitely described by John Ruskin and whose pigeons are world famous. St. Sophia is in Constantinople. And thus we might go on and on. We could find most of these more famous for their finery or architecture or history than for the fullness of the Spirit of God.

Then we go on to other temples of the other religions of the world. There is the great Mosque of the Mohammedans in Damascus, and

the Dome of the Rock in Jerusalem, commonly
called the Mosque of Omar. Then we visit the
Buddhist temples such as the new one just outside the city of Benares, India, erected by an
American woman; to the Swe-di-gon in Ran-
goon, a thousand temples in one. We would see
the temple of Neami in Peiping and many
others in India, China and Japan.

And then there are the other temples of worship to visit, the snake temples, the monkey
temples, the elephant temples and many more
of the Hindus. Then we visit the temples of
Confucius, though they serve not so much religion as philosophy. When one of his pupils asked
about God, he said, "If I do not understand
man whom I have seen, how can I understand
God who is not seen?" Confucius was a phil-
osopher, and his system is not a religion but
a philosophy of life. And yet they have their
temples. But the Spirit of God does not dwell
in them.

Of course the great Bible temple was that of
Solomon, the most magnificent building ever
erected to the honor of God in the name of
religion. I think this is a suggestion and model
for us that God ought to have the best in every
community.

If God should have the best house in which
His people may assemble, and where He may
meet them in their worship, He also ought to
have the very best in the human temple. God's
temple ought to be the purest, finest, cleanest,
best place in the community. And Christian

people ought to be the best people in the world since they are the dwelling place for God.

Now it may be that this verse refers primarily to the spiritual church rather than to the individual Christian, ''Know ye not that ye are the temples of God.'' It, no doubt, refers to both. There are other Scriptures which confirm the position that the individual Christian is meant to be God's dwelling place on Earth.

Let us think of it first as referring to the church, the spiritual body of Christ in which the Holy Spirit dwells. In that light we find here, some very wonderful instructions for Christian workers, ministers, Sunday School teachers, B.Y.P.U. leaders, W.M.U. workers, Brotherhood officers and others. What is it? There are two kinds of temples. One is made of gold, silver and precious stones which abides the ravages of time, the force of the elements and the attack of enemies. The other one is made of wood, hay, stubble and is easily destroyed and falls down.

Now, Christian workers, if you put imperfect material, false teachings, temporary work into the temple of God, it is going to be destroyed. But if you put the gold of genuine Christian character, the silver of benevolent service, and the precious stones of divine truth into the temple of God it will abide.

If all who build the temple of God would only recognize the responsibility of being careful about the kind of material that is put into that temple, they would save much trouble in every

way. We can't build the temple of God out of
the material with which Chambers of Com-
merce and civic clubs and worldly programs
are carried on. We must build it with eternal
and spiritual values of God and His word and
work.

This principle applies also to the individual
character, the kind of person that is built by
our Christian work. I think it applies also to
the kind of individual person who is put into
the spiritual building of God's house.

While in Philadelphia last May speaking for
the Eastern Theological Seminary my attention was drawn across the street to a great
building with numbers of men working on it.
It was a two million dollar hotel that had been
erected a year or so ago and the building in-
spector had condemned it as not safe. Imperfect material had been put into the foundation
and the entire block of the city was jeopardized
by that building.

Whenever an evangelist or pastor or church
worker takes a piece of false material, an un-
redeemed, unregenerated person who has not
been made new by the power of God, and puts
him into the building of the temple of God he
jeopardizes all the interests that are related to
it. Oh, how careful we ought to be here in
building this temple of God.

This principle applies also to the individual
Christian heart and life as the temple of God.

The president of a Christian College had an
only son. This son fell sick and died. When

the funeral service had ended and they started
out, members of his college class were pallbear-
ers. Passing out the door one of them stumbled. It looked as though the casket would fall.
The president said to the boys very quietly and
with dignity, "Careful, young men, careful,
young men, know ye not that you are bearing
the temple of the Holy Ghost."

Careful, young men and young women here
tonight, as you go out of this place, know you
not that you bear about, that you carry with
you the temple of the Holy Ghost. Know ye
not that ye are the temple of God.

Is it right for a Christian to do this, or that,
or the other? We pastors are often asked this
question. Well, I would ask you to put this
test up by the side of that question and answer
it for yourself. If God is living in your heart
and your body is the temple, the sacred temple
of God, what should be the answer as to where
you should go and what you should do? Would
you carry God into those places or go to them
with God in your heart? And I think that question will answer itself for you if you will always remember that you are the temple of the
Holy Ghost.

Now there are three things about a temple
of God that we may consider.

One is that a temple is a purchased and paid
for place. That is, most of them are paid for.
During the last four years one out of 2,284
churches have failed, financially, while one out
of four banks has failed, one out of every

twenty-two industries has failed, one out of forty-four hospitals, one out of every 120 colleges has failed. Only one out of every 2,284 churches has become bankrupt financially. That is the finest business record in the world. If you want your money to be in the safest place in the world, put it into a church. You will have only one chance out of 2,284 to lose it.

Again, the Temple of God is a purchased place, a paid for place, bought for God. "Ye are not your own, ye are bought with a price."

> "Jesus paid it all,
>    All to Him I owe,
>    Sin had left its crimson stain,
>    He washed it white as snow."

These hands, these feet, this body are not mine, Jesus Christ has bought them and paid for them and they belong to Him. I should ask Him about how to use them and where to carry them and I should never disregard His will or His wish in that matter.

Now another thing which we may consider is, that the temple of God is a sanctified place, a set apart place, set apart for specific purposes. That is what the word sanctified means, set apart, holy unto God. Now with that view of it, how awful it is to desecrate a temple, which has been set apart, to the work and worship of God.

The most wonderfully ornate service ever conducted with great crowds and a great choir was the dedication of Solomon's temple on

Mount Moriah in Jerusalem. The longest prayer recorded in the Bible is the prayer of dedication by Solomon by which he set apart the temple of God.

When we dedicated this church house we held a week of special services and on the Lord's day morning we had Dr. George W. Truett come and preach the dedication sermon. The prayer of dedication was offered by the pastor and this place was set apart, holy, sanctified, unto God.

Now, if you and I should pick up the morning paper and read about a band of ruffians who had come into this house of worship of the First Baptist Church of Shreveport, smoking, gambling, committing lust in the house of the First Baptist Church we would all be incensed beyond words or we would weep over it and we would want to go out on a crusade to find those people because they had desecrated a Holy place.

How much more is it wrong to desecrate the temple of God, which temple we are. Shall I smoke? Shall I drink? Shall I eat gluttonously? Shall I over sleep? Shall I under sleep? Shall I over work? Shall I under work? Shall I allow my body to become a prey to disease? Shall I injure it with dope? Answer those questions as though you were answering what should we do with the house of God, with the temple of the Holy Ghost, with the dwelling place of the Most High. I believe it is a solemn, religious, divine obligation for us to keep our body clean, wholesome, sweet, pure, healthy as the dwelling place of God in the world.

And, then, again a temple is a useful place. It has its utilitarian purpose and objective as well as its worshipful and sacred. Jesus announced a great principle when He said, ''The Sabbath was made for man and not man for the Sabbath.'' And the principle can apply to any institution, to the Sabbath, to the government, to the church, to the college, to the kind of business in which we are engaged. They are made for man and not man for them. The constitution of the United States was made for man and not man for the constitution. The test of every institution, the divine test, the Bible test, is, whether or not that institution serves the highest, finest, best interests of humanity. Does it build man's character, does it raise his ideals, does it strengthen one's manhood or womanhood? If it does, it is of God. If it doesn't, it is of the devil and ought to be given up.

Now this church house, sacred as it is, sanctified as it has been made, must serve some practical purpose. These bodies of ours, sanctified temples of the Holy Ghost, must serve. Our feet ought to go every day upon missions of mercy, our hands every day ought to see some kind deed done in the name of our Lord and our body ought to bear the burden and suffering of humanity. They ought to be made useful to the people everywhere for the glory of God and the uplifting of society.

"Know ye not that ye are the temple of God," the sanctuary of the Lord in whom He has a dwelling place. AMEN.

Ephesians 3:16

# Ephesians 3:16

MY PART of this annual student program tonight consists of a brief message from Ephesians 3:16.

"That He would grant you, according to the riches of His glory, to be strengthened with might by His Spirit in the inner man."

If we believe the Bible to be the word of God we cannot have any doubt but that God is interested in our affairs. And we know that God desires the highest and best for our life. In order that we may have the highest and best of life He has designed inner strength for the realization of those ideals and of those things which are of most importance to our character for time and for eternity.

God said to Joshua, "Be strong and of good courage."

The inspiring word said to the young preacher, Timothy, was: "Be strong and of good courage."

The prayers of the apostle Paul for his people and especially for these people in Ephesus, and more particularly for the young people there was this: that they might be "strengthened with might in the inner man."

Your athletic program in college and university provides for the strengthening of your physical powers. Your teachers in the class room provide for the strengthening of your intellec-

tual powers. God has made provision through
His Word, through His Son, Jesus Christ, and
through the Holy Spirit for strengthening your
spiritual powers.

And I am persuaded, my young friends, that
the greatest need is the latter, namely: "That
you may be strengthened with might in the
inner man." The inner man means our spiritual life.

Lack of inner strength, lack of courage, lack
of heroism is an outstanding characteristic of
the age in which we are now living. The tragedy of all tragedies is this — that we have
many small people occupying large positions,
or I might say rattling around in big places
in the world.

Another characteristic is that so many people are filled with so many interests and have
their powers divided and diverted into so many
channels that they exhaust themselves at these
daily rounds of little nothings and have nothing
left on the inside of them for the bigger and
more important things of life. God's divine
word fails to reach them because they cannot
hear the gentle tapping of God's telegraphic
message and the stately stepping of the coming
of the King of Kings. And because they are
unable to recognize the voice of the dove of
peace they lack the power of wise choice and
therefore fall into many hurtful errors.

We are going and going fast and ever faster
but what will we have and be when we get
there? This is a much more important question than how quickly can we get there.

In the races of ancient Greece, the crown of glory was placed upon the brow, not of the one who touched the tape first in his race, but upon the one who touched it first with his torch still burning. A torch was put in the hand of each racer and he must end his race with his torch still burning. That torch is the light of life kindled upon the altar of our hearts and the true object is not to get somewhere quicker than someone else, but to get there with the torch still burning.

You can drive your automobile at 75 miles an hour or ride your airplane at 200 miles an hour and beat the previous record in getting there. But a more important question is what kind of person are you when you reach where you are going?

We now fly from New York to Los Angeles in a few hours in one of our great trans-continental air liners. Our forefathers required many weeks to make the journey in a covered wagon. Are you a better man and a bigger man, a finer woman and a more beautiful character after arriving at high speed than were those who went in the covered wagon?

My friend, Tohoyiko Kagawa, of Japan, now in America speaking to great groups of young people and students all over the country, expressed the same thought in these words: "Present-Day civilization is too shortsighted. Materialistic tendencies have seized the hearts of many of the young men. Because of this, little reliance can be put on their inner power.

They have very little soul-power. People rely too much on the power of the materialistic environment and circumstances.

"I feel that this tendency is one of the most sorrowful currents in this age. We really cannot doubt the surprising activity of the power within; but in spite of experience, people do not believe. When we realize how very bad some environments are, we are made to feel clearly the mighty urge of the inner power.

"I believe that by the strength of the soul it is possible to preserve purity and beauty, even under the very worst living conditions. Through living experiences I came to realize that the fountain-like inner power would not submit to the outer power.

"Stanley Hall, disciple of the great German psychologist, Wundt, is said to have declared that the people who have no morale are hopeless. Some nations, because of habits of smoking opium, taking cocaine, or drinking whisky, lose their precious morale, and degenerate. For example, 'China is degenerating because of opium,' declared Sun Yat Sen. The American Indians have degenerated because of drink and syphilis, and the same may be said of the Ainu (the aborigines of Japan). In the autumn of 1928 I traveled around in the Hokkaido, where many of these Ainu live, and carefully examined the conditions of these people. I found that the soul-force of many of these natives had disappeared. How I did pity them."

Two persons may walk down the street of our city tomorrow morning, pass the door of an open liquor house, one of them fall a prey to the evil, and the other stand majestically above it. What is the difference? Not a difference in governmental system, not a difference in educational opportunities, not a difference in environment. The difference in those persons is the difference in the inner power that dwells in their hearts.

We may say, therefore, that all governmental systems, all college programs and plans of education, all institutions for the social service of the people, all our homes and our churches must in their primal responsibility build bigger and better men and women on the inside, if we are to save the things that are best. The outer and material forces have developed so much faster than the inner and spiritual forces that they have gotten out of control and are liable to become man's enemy instead of servant.

Let us develop self control, that is the object of true religion. We will have a great deal of discussion and many ahs! and ohs! and wails over the return of legalized liquor by the repeal of the 18th amendment. And we are crying out for some political system, for an educational program which will prevent liquor from destroying our youth. May I say that the first place to stop the sale of liquor is on the inside of each and every individual. Prohibition by an external force imposed upon people from outside without having their inside sanction and support has already failed in the past. Successful prohibition must come from an internal spiritual power which will deliver each individual from drink.

The way to stop the sale of all liquor is for everybody to stop using it. If we are to prevent the use of liquor, opium, drugs, licentiousness, crime, iniquity of all sorts, it will be done by building the power within us. The forces from without are not going to be able to accomplish it. Oh, that you young students may be strengthened with might in the inner man!

Great world leaders who have captured kingdoms and established empires have manifested self control. More power is manifested on the inside of one in the control of his own spirit than is manifested when one takes a city. The power of God's divine Son and the light of God's divine truth in the brain and blood and nerves of men and women, taking possession of them and giving them strength by which to control conduct is mightier than all external forces.

We have seen the heat of hell burn in a soul and do its devastating work. And then we have seen the healing power of God's grace come into that soul and strengthen it with a vitality which enables it to withstand all temptations. It is the same divine power by which Jesus Christ was raised from the dead. And it is the same power which is offered to each and every one of you, power for enduring, power for con flicts, power for service, power for overcoming

But we have not this power because we do not ask for it. And we do not ask because we really do not want it. If we want to be saved from the sins of the world we can be saved. This inner power will manifest itself in a magnificent way to the glory of God and the good of the people.

I think one of the most striking illustrations that I have ever come across of the impotency of physical forces in the presence of inner strength is Bishop Fisher's description of non-resistance in India. Gandhi, the great pacifist, had taught his people not to live by the force of outside mechanical power but to live by the strength of inner vitality.

## The Fighting Pacifist

*"Rags! Rags! shall I wear*
*Straw! Straw! Shall I eat*
*For the sake of thy life,*
*My motherland.*

*"Into the street*
*'Neath trampling feet*
*I cast all fame,*
*To serve thy name*
*O heart's dear flame*
*My Motherland."*

"Somewhere behind a closed window in Bombay, a woman was singing this battle hymn of passive resistance. But in the streets of the city there was no singing, only silence.

"The terrible silence of India! I have experienced it. Thousands of soft feet slipping
through the warm dust, pliant sandals and slip-
pers making no sound on the pavement. No
sound; no voice. You were alone on a street
corner of Bombay; then, suddenly you turned
your head, and all India was there at your
shoulder. All day long on June 21st, 1930, the
crowds of Indians had been gathering against
the strict orders of the constabulary that there
must be no national meetings or parades. The
people had begun coming in the early morning,
yet so silent was their approach that before the
government knew it, every square yard of the
main avenue of Bombay was covered by a vast
human sea of bodies.

"Silence, absolute, menacing, more terrible
than trumpets. It was only when the police put
up machine guns on the street corner and
threatened the mob if they did not disperse,
that India began its march.

" 'If you come as far as the corner, we will
shoot!' "

"The message was brought to the man heading the parade, by an armed soldier, the clatter
of his horse's feet beating defiantly against the
menacing quiet.

" 'We will fire to kill!' "

" 'Very well, fire.' "

"With a sigh of released patience, the crowd
began to move slowly, relentlessly, proudly,
toward the deadly corner. The leaders held
their heads high . . . till the rat tat tat of the

machine guns sent them bowing awkwardly into the dust. The English had fired as they had
promised.

"Still there was little confusion; only the
gasps of the wounded and dying, their clumsy
twitchings in the street. The leaders were gone.
Would the crowd march on? Silently, slowly,
yet as certainly as an incoming tide that cannot be stemmed the next in rank stepped over
the dead and came toward the guns. Once more
the stutter of guns, the gleam of metal under
a blazing sun. More men whirled, fell, cough-
ing blood, clutched helplessly at their bursting
stomachs, and then fell dead. But still the
steady stream came on, more and more men,
more and more women; stern, implacable, ready
to die. It could not be true! But it was. It
was a scene out of Dante's hell, imagined not
to be believed.

" 'I say. This is terrible. We can't do this,
Captain!'

"It was the young English lieutenant speaking. 'Can't we move the guns up to the next
corner?'

"There was sweat on the Captain's fore-
head.

" 'Yes. Move them up. And warn the Indians
that if they stop now we will not shoot. But
they must not come to the next corner.'

"The crowd was told . . . but it still marched
on. Guns were hurried to another corner. Still
the crowd swept silently forward. What was

to be done? All Bombay could not be slaughtered. 'What can we do to get you to stop?' the English officer called.

"The low voice of the Indian leader stirred the thick layer of Indian silence for the first time.

" 'So long as you point your guns at us, we will march. Rescind your order against our meeting, take away your guns . . . and we will disperse.'

" 'But that would be to surrender!'

" 'Very well, then. We will march till every one of these thousands is dead.'

"It was India demanding a chance to be heard. The guns were removed, the crowd melted away like magic, lifting up the wounded and burying their dead. But the voice of silent India had been heard on her own streets of Bombay."

And may God strengthen you students with might in the inner man by the power of the indwelling Christ and by the power of His eternal Word that you may be filled with all the fullness of God.

Colossians 3:16

# Colossians 3:16

CONTINUING our explorations and excavations in the three-sixteens of the New Testament, we find ourselves in the third chapter of Colossians, this morning. When I was first invited to Shreveport nearly 25 years ago, I was preaching a series of sermons from this book of Colossians. It has been a rich book to me through all the years. It deals with the profound things of the heart's relationship to God. It sets out the supremacy and sufficiency of Jesus Christ. We will find in this verse sixteen of chapter three a very vital revelation. I shall read from the fifth verse in order that we may catch up the theme and carry it on to the sixteenth.

Colossians 3:5-16:

Mortify therefore your members which are upon the earth; fornication, uncleanness, inordinate affection, evil concupiscence, and covetousness, which is idolatry:

For which things' sake the wrath of God cometh on the children of disobedience:

In the which ye also walked some time, when ye lived in them.

But now ye also put off all these; anger, wrath, malice, blasphemy, filthy communication out of your mouth.

Lie not one to another, seeing that ye have put off the old man with his deeds;

And have put on the new man, which is renewed in knowledge after the image of him that created him:

Where there is neither Greek nor Jew, circumcision nor uncircumcision, Barbarian, Scythian, bond nor free: but Christ is all, and in all.

Put on therefore, as the elect of God, holy and beloved, bowels of mercies, kindness, humbleness of mind, meekness, longsuffering;

Forbearing one another, and forgiving one another, if any man have a quarrel against any: even as Christ forgave you, so also do ye.

And above all these things put on charity, which is the bond of perfectness.

And let the peace of God rule in your hearts, to the which also ye are called in one body; and be ye thankful.

Let the word of Christ dwell in you richly in all wisdom; teaching and admonishing one another in psalms and hymns and spiritual songs, singing with grace in your hearts to the Lord.

This figure of speech of disrobing and dressing ought to help us wonderfully because we do it so often, at least twice a day. When we do this for our physical body we should do it for our spiritual being, putting off anger, wrath, malice, taking them off as a garment, laying them aside, then putting on mercy, kindness, humbleness of mind, meekness, long-suffering, forbearing, etc.

I want to thank the choir for the cooperation given in the selection of the music for this morning. It is in perfect harmony with this message. It was selected during my absence last week. There must have been divine guidance. And that is what church music is meant to do as we shall see presently — to build up our thinking for the message of God.

"In Psalms and hymns and spiritual songs, with melody in your heart as unto the Lord."

I saw a little boy a while ago doing what I wish all of you would do during the singing of the hymns. His face was in the hymn book, his eyes on the words, and his lips and voice were doing the best they could. He did not appear to be conscious of anybody or anything else around him. He was singing with all his might, as if this whole service depended on him. I wish everybody would be like that at every service.

Music is an art, a kind of infallible speech by which we are led to view eternity and to catch a glimpse of the infinite. It may be infinite suffering or infinite joy, it may be infinite evil or infinite good. That depends upon the origin of the music, the character of the music and depends upon the attitude of the singer toward it.

This morning we are to consider the ministry of music in the churches of Christ. One very striking thing you learn in a journey around the world is that heathenism has no hymn books. They have weird chants, dirges of despair, but no joyful, delightful, victorious music. The fact of the business is the heathen religions have no congregational worship. They only come with their offerings to appease the wrath of their god who wants to do them evil, and to try to keep the evil spirits off as long as possible. There is a sadness in their chant as of a hope unrealized. It breaks one's heart to think of the darkness in which they live.

But Christianity is the religion of music, of sunshine, of gladness, of flowers, of fragrance, of joy, of peace, of power, of triumphs over the world, the flesh and the devil. Therefore Christian music has a note that we do not find anywhere else in the world. It has an intellect which is satisfying because of its conception of God. One who is righteous, just, merciful, compassionate, even self-sacrificing. In Christian music God is revealed in the person of Jesus Christ. In Christ God has come to the earth for the redemption of humanity from sickness, suffering, sorrow and sin. It gives to those who accept Christ victory over broken hearts, helpless hands, and over all the enemies of the human race. Christian music brings joy to the heart with the hope of everlasting life, even when one walks through the valley of the shadow of death.

The second Bible song is a hymn of rededication found in Nehemiah. Then come the songs of David, praises to God as recorded in the Psalms. In Job, in the Song of Solomon and in Chronicles we have other great hymns.

But we do not hear the full open diapason of heaven's music until we reach the New Testament where the angels' choir breaks forth singing glory to God in the highest, and on earth peace, goodwill toward men. Moving on through the Gospel stories in search of music we come to the end of Christ's career on earth. We find Him and His disciples in an upper room on the night of betrayal and the one before He was to die. What are they doing? Are they moaning and groaning and chanting some weird dirge of despair? No! They are singing. They sang a hymn and went out. What did they sing? Probably Psalm 18. While this song looked forward to the cross, it was a song of victory, of triumph.

Only Christian music can produce that sort of thing in the human heart. And only a Christian heart can produce that sort of music.

In the Acts we find other triumphant hymns, most notable among them being the song of Paul and Silas in the midnight jail. This was a song that burst the prison doors and loosed the disciples from their shackles, and brought salvation to the jailer and his house.

And then the song of Moses and the Lamb recorded in the last book of the Bible, Revelation, is a grand finale to heaven's music and is a welcome to the coming King. Even so come quickly, Lord Jesus.

So from the second book of the Bible, Exodus, to the Revelation, there are constantly recurring bursts of song.

They are all psalms and songs and hymns of joy, of praise, of victory, and of hope.

There are four things which this text says about Christian music.

> Let the word of Christ dwell in you richly in all wisdom; teaching and admonishing one another in psalms and hymns and spiritual songs, singing with grace in your hearts to the Lord. (Colossians 3:16)

The origin of music is in the heart. The kind of music which comes forth depends upon the kind of heart from which it comes. Nowhere is the statement "As a man thinketh in his heart so is he," more real than in the music he produces. The lips speak forth the things that are in the heart.

Music is an elemental method of expression. From the very beginning of the human race men have essayed music. But not until that spirit in man was joined to the very words of the book of God was there ever any music worthy the name.

Then under the genius of Handel, Mendelssohn and others like them it burst forth upon the world in immortal oratorios. Let the word of Christ dwell richly in your heart, then you can sing psalms and hymns and spiritual songs unto the Lord.

This phrase "the word of Christ," may mean either one of two things. It may mean Christ's word which He gave to us. It may mean the word about Christ which was given to us by the inspired writers. In either case Christ is the center of the thought. Now, let the word of Christ dwell in you, in your heart, and there will be melody and music of the highest and holiest sort.

This word, "dwell in you," I found to be very interesting. I enjoy chasing down the genealogy of words. This word is one which is used with reference to housekeeping, and so here is what it means. Let the word of Christ be welcome in your heart. Let the word of Christ find hospitality on the inside of you. Let it set up housekeeping there. Let the word of Christ find lodging, permanent residence in your heart. The word of Christ is abroad in the earth, seeking housing and there is a great housing shortage. It does not find sufficient residences in which to set up housekeeping. We are urged to provide more housing facilities in our hearts for Christ's Word.

Now the phrase goes further than that and suggests that the hospitality which we give to the Word of Christ when it enters our hearts for housekeeping, shall ascribe to it, not the position of a servant, not even the position of a guest, but rather the position of a Master. The Word of Christ in the heart which has been given welcome and hospitality and which has set up housekeeping there is to rule and be master of all that goes on in that house and especially is it to control the music that is there.

Oh! my! suppose Christ should appear in our homes? A lot of the junk which we have on the piano or in the music seat would have to go out the back door. A lot of the jazzy, jiggity junk on the radio would be immediately shut off. The Word of Christ could and would not dwell there. Let the Word of Christ take up residence, even a permanent position of authority in your heart.

I found myself on the train without anything to read except a very modern magazine. I wondered if I could find anything in that for a sermon. I soon came across an article the first sentence of which was this: "Where to live will always be a problem." Then the article went on to say that everybody lives in some sort of house. For an Eskimo it is an igloo. For the Indian it is a tepee. For us it may be a log hut, a cottage, a Spanish bungalow, or a colonial mansion.

Upon entering a new house the "house warming" is a custom practiced by all. It is an invitation to friends to bring a gift which will make the new home more comfortable and happy. The Indians call it making whoopee. Pagans open their new house with dancing and drinking and eating. Christians open their new house by dedicating it to God (Deut. 20:5).

Now, when the heart is opened for occupancy and the Word of Christ comes in, it brings gifts, too. Christ's Word brings gifts to make the house more comfortable and livable. Those gifts are psalms and hymns and spiritual songs.

Psalms and hymns and spiritual songs are to be used in the home of the heart in four ways:

First, by intelligently comprehending their meaning;

Second, with warm hearted acceptance of their authority;

Third, with enjoyable exercise; and

Fourth, by industriously presenting them to others.

Here, then, is a test of the condition of our heart—What kind of music has been given hospitality and what kind do we enjoy exercising and giving forth to others. I know of no other standard by which we can better measure the height or depth of our own likes and dislikes.

Church music should be didactic as well as inspirational. Inspiration without some solid substance is likely to leave one flat. Church music should teach divine truth as well as inspire conduct. To teach requires subject matter and Christian music contains some of the best subject matter. Occasionally, however, we hear some music in our churches which has no rightful place among God's people and especially in God's house. I once heard and saw one of these abominations of desolation standing where he should not, otherwise known as a "live wire," "spizerinktum," "pep-'em-up," song leader, direct a congregation in singing with a jazz tune, "A little down duckling went down to a pond."

We not only improve others when we teach
truths by psalms and hymns but we improve
ourselves. The communication of knowledge
confirms the teacher. The teacher always learns
more when teaching than he does when studying. To admonish one another is a constantly
recurring exhortation in the Holy Scriptures,
and we are urged to do it in our psalms, hymns
and spiritual songs.

We are commanded to bear one another's
burdens and so fulfill the law of Christ. How
can this be done any better than in our psalms
and hymns and spiritual songs? By our hymns
we build ourselves together into one thought,
in Christ.

Differences of opinion and confessions of
faith are lost in singing. None of us ever stop
to raise the question, for example, when we sing
the hymns and spiritual songs of the great
hymn writers, whether the composer was a
Baptist, a Methodist, a Presbyterian or what
not. When we sing such songs as "Come ye
that love the Lord" we do not raise the question as to whether he was a Presbyterian.
When we sing Wesley's "O for a thousand
tongues to sing our great Redeemer's praise,"
we do not ask if he was a Methodist. Metho-
dists and Presbyterians sing the hymns and
tunes written by Baptists just as lustily as do
the Baptists themselves. Listen to a Methodist
sing "How Firm a Foundation," "My Hope is
Built on Nothing Else," "Majestic Sweetness," "Shall We Gather at the River?"

"Blest Be the Tie that Binds," "Come Thou Fount," and hundreds of others written by Baptists. And all of them sing the Unitarian's hymn: "Nearer My God to Thee."

When the soul is touched by the spirit of God and led to sing hymns and spiritual songs which teach the Word of God, then it finds itself in harmony with all others which have had a similar experience. That is a true objective of music in the churches of Christ — the building up of Christian character and faith and hope and love.

The Apostle Paul is contrasting that kind of music with the music of these pagan and heathen peoples before their conversion.

The Greeks were particularly devoted to the art of music. But their songs were songs of jest, social ribaldry and even of lust. Their songs were songs of the street, songs of the siren voices, of houses of shame.

Now, Paul says to them: "If the word of Christ has entered your heart, put those songs away. They are destructive of character, of ideals, and of the soul. Put them away and sing the hymns and spiritual songs which will build up Christian character and life."

I fear that some of the old pagan life has come over into our church music. I have had people who formerly lived the ways of the world before they became Christians tell me that some of the church music stirs the same old feelings of lust and sin in their blood.

Music that belongs to the dance hall and the house of prostitution has absolutely no place in the house of God.

While in China I noticed that the Chinese Christians sing the hymns of our American churches and use the English tunes. So I said to them: "I think each people ought to produce its own music for the Lord. I don't urge you Chinese Christians to try to be like American Christians. You should be Chinese Christians."

Christianity should take root in the life of the people as they are and produce in them what God would have them to be. I said, "Why haven't you produced hymns and music of your own?" The Chinese answer was invariably: "Practically all of our Chinese music has been the music of the street, music of lust and of evil and if we brought that music into our church houses it would be a reminder to those who have been converted from heathenism, of their old life, and we ought not to do that." I wonder if that isn't done too much among us American Christians. I wish we would always observe that same consideration in our Church music. For my part I hope that we never again hear, in this church, any music or tune which will remind any one of evil experiences.

Listen to this from Sir Henry Coward, and I quote it with approval: "The Academy of Music . . . is a bulwark against, and an antidote to the atavistic, semibarbaric, banging and swaying, humming and strumming, irritating

St. Vitus' dance, persistently exploited by some of the sons of Belial as music.''

The nearer heathen you are the more you live in the flesh, the world, and the devil, the more you will like that kind of music. The more you live in the Spirit of God and by the power of Christ the more you will love spiritual hymns and songs and psalms. Away with all music which tears down character, on with music which builds better things into our life. Let us be done with music which stirs only physical emotions, and seek more of that which creates spiritual experiences. Much of the ''whoop-it-up'' evangelistic music is nothing more or less than appeals to the physical senses and has no relationship to spiritual vitality and ideals.

With Christ in the heart, for the religion of Christ is a great religion, the heart will pour forth torrents of music ''unto the Lord.'' We can make no melody in our own heart, nor admonish others, nor can we honor God unless we ourselves have been suitably affected by the words which we sing or the music which we play.

Let us all emulate that boy whom I saw a while ago, singing, not to you, nor to me, but out of his heart unto the Lord.

We hear of concert artists being advertised as having sung before this or that king or queen. That is wonderful publicity. But you and I may advertise that we have sung before the King of kings and Lord of lords. We sing our hymns and spiritual songs with melody in our heart unto the Lord.

II Timothy 3:16

# II Timothy 3:16

W E CONTINUE our flights over the mountain ranges of God's revelations pausing here and there on the three-sixteens of the New Testament. For this morning we land for a while at II Timothy 3:16. This is the counsel of an old minister to a young preacher.

"And that from a child thou hast known the Holy Scriptures, which are able to make thee wise unto salvation through faith, which is in Christ Jesus.

"All scripture is given by inspiration of God and is profitable for doctrine, for reproof, for correction, for instruction in righteousness:

"That the man of God may be perfected, thoroughly furnished unto all good works."

The sixteenth verse is, "All Scripture is given by inspiration of God and is profitable for doctrine, for reproof, for correction, for instruction in righteousness."

When I came home last night, Mrs. Dodd was sitting alone in the library. She looked up with a smile of welcome and I said, "When did you hear from God?" The smile went away and she appeared puzzled at such a strange question and said, "What is the matter with you?" I said, "I am studying my sermon for tomorrow and I think that will be my opening sentence. It will secure attention for my subject. If I had come in and asked you: 'Have you heard from Lucile?' you would have said, 'Yes, here is a letter which has just come this afternoon. Let me read it to you.' 'Have you heard from Martha?' 'Yes, she just called up on the telephone from New Orleans.' ''

Well, "When did you hear from God?" Why not answer that question as you did the others. The Bible is God's message to His children.

Why not open it and say: "I have heard from Him today and here is what He says."

"Is there any word from the Lord?" Yes:

"All Scripture is given by inspiration of God and is profitable for doctrine, for reproof, for correction, and instruction in righteousness."

The Bible is His message, His word, His truth, His expressed desire for our life. Here it is; let me read you part of it and tell you what He says. Here we can find all that He has to say to us.

Let us pause awhile at II Timothy 3:16.

This verse says two things about the Bible. It says first that everything in this Book is inspired of God, all Scriptures. All Scriptures (from *scripto*, "to write," "the writings,") are inspired of God.

The second thing said, is that the inspired writings of God are for our profit, they are profitable. It then specifies some of the things for which those inspired Scriptures are profitable.

Let us look at these two things for a while. First, think of the Bible as a Book written by inspiration of God.

There are three views concerning the origin of the Bible.

The Bible came to us by intellectual illumination, say some.

It came by mechanical dictation, say others.

It came by spiritual inspiration, say others.

I heard a minister say, "I know the Bible is inspired because it inspires me." Well, Kipling inspires me and Shakespeare inspires me and Bacon and Tennyson inspire me, but that does not mean that they or their writings were inspired of God. They may have been intellectually illuminated, but they were not inspired. There is a great difference between intellectual illumination and spiritual inspiration.

There is also the idea that the Bible came by mechanical dictation just as a business man would dictate to his stenographer word for word. But this theory cannot explain the full meaning of the Bible. It is more than word. It is more than mechanics, law or form. The Bible is spirit, it is life.

We cannot study the Bible as we would study other books from a mere intellectual standpoint and get the full meaning of it. We may get all the Greek texts and commentaries and word studies for our Bible study, just as a botanist would dissect a flower or as a physician or surgeon would operate on the body. Yet that does not disclose to us the Bible's full meaning. There is something more in the body than organs. There is life, there is spirit. There is far more in a flower than chemical compounds, there is fragrance. Unless we find fragrance, spirit, life, in the Bible we have not found what God would have us get out of it. No, mechanical dictation cannot explain the Bible.

There remains the faith that the Bible came by spiritual inspiration. What is that? The Bible itself says: "Holy men of God wrote as they were moved by the Holy Ghost."

Now, this spiritual inspiration has to do with three things.

First, inspiration is a direct communication from God. "God spake all these words." "The word of the Lord came unto," so and so saying. Expressions like these are found 580 times in the five books of law, 518 times in the twelve books of history and 1502 times in the books of prophecy: 2600 times in all it is said in the Old Testament, and 525 times in the New Testament, making in all 3,125 times that it is said the Bible is a direct communication from God.

"When did you hear from God?" "Is there any word from the Lord?" Any time you read the Bible you hear from God, for it is God's word communicated through man to man. "Holy men of old wrote as they were moved, as they were borne along, by the Holy Ghost." When men of God were borne along by His Spirit and His message was delivered to them they wrote it and we have it here. Jeremiah is an illustration of this. Baruch was asked of the people, "How did you get these words? How did you get this message?" Baruch said,

"He spoke them out of his mouth and I wrote them down." I imagine as he looked upon the face of Jeremiah, who was in contact with God, he saw something he had never seen and heard something he had never heard. He wrote down the words which God gave to his servant Jeremiah. God gave the message to Jeremiah, he spoke it and Baruch wrote it. God speaks in heaven, Jeremiah translates it into human language and Baruch writes it and God's message appears in His book.

I was going through the great Union Station in St. Louis, and I saw a pen writing on a scroll of paper. There was no one there and I stopped to look at this strange thing. I sought a guard and asked him, "What is this thing?" He said, "The station master on the fourth floor of this building, in his office, is writing instructions. Through electric connections the writing is appearing on the paper for the man on the ground floor, for whom it was intended." Something like that is the way we got our Bible. God took up His pen in heaven and wrote, and through the electric current of divine inspiration to the heart and hand of His chosen human instrument, the words and letters and sentences began to take shape on a scroll on earth and this is God's communication to the world.

The second thing about spiritual inspiration is the selection of material. That is illustrated in the historical books of the Bible. The Bible is the record of God's dealings with humanity. He does not write biography as we do. Some of the greatest characters of all time are dismissed with one sentence, and some of the greatest events of all history are dismissed with one word. Yet twenty-seven chapters are given to the tabernacle alone. What does that mean? It means that the Bible is a Book of God's dealings with humanity and only that is written which has bearing upon the record of relationship between God and man.

We find this illustrated in the New Testament. John says: "These things are written that ye might believe that Jesus is the Christ and that believing ye might have life in His name." John had said, "If the things Jesus did and said were all written in a book, the world could not contain them." But the things recorded here were chosen out of the vast amount of available material, for the purpose of showing that Christ is the Son of God.

God, Himself, prepared the blue prints for the entire canon of scriptures. As that blue print came to its completion, God realized that no one human brain, no one mind, no one person, could carry it all. If the current of God's thought had been turned through one human brain, it would have burned it up. No one individual could have contained so much. So God separated His thought into sections and sent each one through different individuals. He sent this part of the blue print to Moses, and this to David, and this to Isaiah, and this to Paul, and this to Peter, and this to John, and asked them to furnish that material according to the specifications of the particular page of the blue prints. When each and every one completed his task they were all brought together and that became the Bible.

Then again, may I point out that God's providential preservation of the Bible through nearly four thousand years of the world's history and that against the two greatest enemies, namely the ravages of time and the fury of enemies is strong evidence of its divine inspiration. Scientific books are out of date within ten years. Doctors would no more follow the books of 25 years ago than they would stick their faces in fire. These books are out of date. The Bible is nearly four thousand years old, yet as fresh this morning as the snow that blankets the earth or as the sunlight that came upon the dawn. All things earthly and material change into new shapes and forms, but the ravages of time have done nothing to ruin a single gem of beauty in the Word of God. The frantic furies of enemies have broken down this form of government and that form of economics and they are constantly changing. Sometimes a friendly force comes in. The human systems and institutions are constantly being changed. But there has been found no need of change in the Bible because the eternal element in it persists. The life of God is in it the same yesterday, and today, and forever.

Last night I read again the story of the burning of those books of vile literature in Ephesus. I asked what were the names of those books?

I don't know. Do you? Does anybody know the
titles of those books? Who were the publishers?
What did those books discuss? Can you tell
me? No! Why? Because they were light, temporary, inconsequential. Nobody cared to re-
produce them. Contrast this with the effort of
the Roman Emperor Diocletian who ordered
the gathering of all Bibles that they might be
destroyed. They were burned. Yet, I have a
copy of the Bible today. Four hundred million
copies of this Book are issued by the Bible
societies every year. The printing press which
turned out the works of Voltaire, the one which
printed his prophecy that within a hundred
years all Bibles would be gone, was purchased
by the Geneva Bible Society and now prints
thousands of copies of the Bible every year.
The Bible lives when other books die. There
must be a divine life within it, a spirit which
cannot be destroyed by the physical forces of
the world.

Now the fact that the Scriptures and science
are in thorough agreement concerning the universe is strong testimony to their common
origin. God's works and God's words are in
complete harmony. There is no conflict between
science and the Bible. Science confirms the
Bible. The Bible actually appeals to science for
confirmation. It appeals to anthropology, or
the science of man, and says: "What is man
that thou art mindful of him, or the son of
man that thou visitest him?" It appeals to astronomy, or the science of the heavens, and

says, "The heavens declare the glory of God and the firmament showeth his handiwork." It appeals to geology and says, "Call you to the earth and it shall teach thee." It appeals to biology and says, "What is thy life?" It appeals to chemistry and says, "Hast thou considered the treasures of the snow?" Look out there at the beautiful snow which blankets the earth this morning and let it tell you of God's grace which cleanses human hearts whiter than snow.

Again let us notice how the Bible commends itself to the mightiest minds of all times. There is something about the Bible that challenges, stimulates, that strengthens, that appeals, to the soundest intellects. And it secures the attention from the highest and the best.

The whole world is in grief at the present moment over the death of King George of England. He was one of the most beloved sovereigns of the Empire and one of the most widely respected rulers of the world. I wonder how much his love of the Bible had to do with this? He was a daily reader of the Holy Scriptures. He said: "It is my confident hope that my subjects may never cease to cherish their noble inheritance in the English Bible, which, in a secular aspect is the first of national treasures and is in its spiritual significance the most valuable thing that this world affords." In the hour of death I wonder if he did not realize the truth of that last part of his statement. "The most valuable thing this world affords."

We have just been celebrating the 129th anniversary of the birth of Robert E. Lee. He was one of the purest, whitest souled men this world ever had. He was a very courageous person, but one to whom no scandal was ever attached. Here is what he said; "The Bible is a book in comparison with which all others in my eyes are of minor importance, and which in all my perplexities and distresses has never failed to give me light and strength." I wonder if that is not the explanation of why the biographers found no stain on this great character. One of them said he was a "man whom the triumphs of life never made vain nor the defeats never destroyed." Rudyard Kipling died last week. His mental vitality has stirred more red blood cells than any other poet's. He was inspired by the Word of God. His *Recessional* is perhaps the best example of this fact. "Lord God of hosts be with us yet, lest we forget, lest we forget."

And now I have given most of the time to the origin of the Bible and there is only a scant moment left for the last word concerning the object of the Bible.

The Bible is not just a vague revelation, it is a practical, useful thing for every day living. It is profitable for doctrine, that is for teaching, for instruction. It is not for teaching science or philosophy or literature, or history, but religion. Not to tell how the heavens go, but how to go to heaven, not to tell about the age of rocks, but to tell of the rock of ages, not to tell about the lilies of the valley, but the Lily of the valley, the Bright and Morning Star, the Rose of Sharon, the Water of Life. It is profitable for teaching about God, man and salvation, about sin, about heaven, and hell. The man who neglects the Word of God robs his soul of the highest and best teaching on the subjects of greatest consequence.

The Bible is profitable for reproof, for convincing us of the errors of our way, for convincing us of our sin and weakness. It is God's moral standard of what we ought to be. When we measure our lives by God's standard we discard our own. The Bible is our standard of morals. It is profitable for correction. It isn't intended simply to convince us of our error or our folly, but to guide us in the right way.

The Bible is for training in uprightness; "for instruction in right doing," for moral discipline. Proper conduct in life and the highest improvement of the soul cannot be secured outside of the Bible. The Bible will train in righteousness, in social policy, in economics, and for the improvement of all human affairs. Every speaker, lecturer, writer, preacher, and teacher is now discussing the subject of how confused the world is. Who knows which way to go? If there is one thing above another that characterizes the time in which we now live, it is the confusion in which we find ourselves. There is one path, one light, one way which we have not fully tested. It is the way of righteousness revealed to us in the Book of God. It came to us direct through divine inspiration from His wisdom and His heart, for our good and guidance.

If every school, if every social and political power, if every educational and economic group would stop still right where they are and pause for a while to search the Word of God and to pray: "Guide us, oh Thou Great Jehovah, guide us in Thy way of truth and life everlasting," we would find ourselves together again with a united purpose, with a unity of thought that we do not have now and can never have as long as we reject the wisdom of God and try to follow human, temporary expedients for the control of our world order.

Search the Scriptures, they are they that testify of Christ.

II Peter 3:16

# II Peter 3:16

THIS second epistle of Peter was written some 30 odd years after the death of Christ. It was sent to the five Roman provinces of Asia Minor to the end that the Christians there might be saved from false interpretations of the Scriptures by the Gnostics.

Not only was Peter very much concerned about this matter but the Apostles Paul and John showed anxiety also. The Epistles to the Ephesians and Colossians reveal the great concern in the heart of Paul and the I Epistle of John opens his heart to us on this question. These three apostles made direct answer, to the atheistic, literalistic, legalistic and other false teachers who were undermining the faith of the Christians.

When we observe the anxiety and deep concern of these great men of God for the faith of their followers we can but marvel at the indifference of some present-day preachers and teachers. Sometimes they sneer at the, "Faith once for all delivered to the Saints." They take the position that it does not matter much what one believes just so he lives right. They seem to forget that right thinking and right believing and right living are inseparably bound together.

Orthodoxy literally means straight thinking, and straight thinking is usually followed by straight living. Heterodoxy is literally crooked thinking and crooked thinking is usually followed by crooked living. "As a man thinketh in his heart, so is he."

David said, "I believe, therefore, I have spoken." What one believes about the ten commandments will usually determine one's attitude and conduct toward those ten commandments. If it is a matter of indifference as to whether one believes them or not or accepts them as authoritative or not, it is a matter of indifference as to whether one lives up to them or not.

One can not think crooked and live straight. Character and conduct must stand, or fall together. True teaching produces true character. False teaching produces false character. This is why Paul, John and Peter wrote to the Christians of Asia Minor urging them to stand by the gospel of Christ and warning them to avoid the false philosophies of the agnostics. "Paul foresaw at Miletus these wolves who would ravish the sheep."

The apostles are following the whole tenor of the scriptures in warning against false teachers.

The Bible has a great deal to say about unfaithful ministers, false shepherds, false prophets, false teachers, corrupt priests.

The Bible describes them as blind, ignorant, dumb dogs, sleepers, lying down, loving to slumber, greedy, looking to their own interests rather than to the people's, selfish, drunkards, pleasure seekers, wolves in sheep's clothing, scatterers of the sheep, leading lost sheep astray, covetous, deceivers, traffickers in men, vain, boasters, seducers, enticers, wanton, abusers of liberty, corrupt, mercenary teachers and sinful imitators.

Bible writers said all of these things about false teachers and more. If they could have thought of more words they no doubt would have used them too. This is the reason Peter wrote this epistle. He was trying to stir up their minds by way of remembrance, and their hearts by way of affection and their convictions by way of confirmation to straight thinking, holy loving and honorable living.

In the second place it is interesting to note here the attitude of Peter toward Paul. They had been fellow laborers for some years now. Paul refers to the fact that when he was converted he went to Jerusalem and spent fifteen days with Peter. I should like to know how far they agreed or disagreed. I wish I might have listened to their conversation. They must have walked and talked much through the streets of Jerusalem, out to the Mount of Olives, to Calvary and to the Tomb. This was Paul's theological Seminary. Paul and Peter had their differences as men of strong mentality, personality and convictions will at times.

On one occasion Paul said, "I had to take Peter to task on this thing. I had to reprove him to his face because he was wrong." A man is not always your enemy because he disagrees with you, reproves you, and seeks to correct you.

Peter was a sensitive person, but he never resented Paul's reproof as a personal affront. They often spoke of each other in a very affectionate manner.

Much of our Christian trouble, scisms, divisions and new denominations, which all sensible people deeply deplore, start from personal differences between the teachers or leaders in the churches or the denomination.

Paul and Peter give us a fine example of proper conduct when personal differences occur. Whatever their personal feelings toward each other they never allowed that to affect the work of the Lord. They never allowed that to affect their attitude and conduct toward the Kingdom of God. What a lesson for all of us! Disagree if we must, debate it out if we will, but never allow it to come into the church or denomination or into the Kingdom of God to create trouble and division in the House of the Lord.

Here, again, is another exceedingly important thing—Peter puts the Apostle Paul and his epistles on a par with the Old Testament characters and their writings. It is definitely stated that the men who wrote the Old Testament Scriptures did so because they were moved by the Holy Ghost. That is a clear cut statement of the divine inspiration of the scriptures. Holy men of old were borne along by the Holy Ghost in their thinking and writing of the Holy Scriptures.

In I Thessalonians 5:27, and Colossians 4:16 it is definitely stated that the Apostle Paul is on the same basis as the Old Testament writers, that is to say his writings were inspired by the Holy Ghost. Peter goes one step further and puts their words on a par in divine origin and authority with the words of the Lord Jesus Christ.

Now that may sound almost like blasphemy to some supersensitive ears. But, just you wait a minute. I bring this in here because there is a school of thought today which seeks to put Christ over against Paul and Christ over against Peter to their discredit. They set up Christ's teaching as divine and authoritative over against that of the Apostles as human and temporary. But that is a false position. What do I mean? I mean that the words of these apostles were inspired by the Holy Ghost and the words of Jesus Christ were inspired by the Holy Ghost and that coming from the same source, from the same power, from the same author, they are equally divine and equally authoritative.

In the next place, let us see what Peter is driving at in this 3:16.

There are three things to be seen here.

First his statement that Paul wrote some things which are hard to be understood.

Second the fact that there are unstable and unlearned Christians in every Church.

Third the sad truth that they wrest, twist and misinterpret the Scriptures to the destruction of themselves and others.

We have no difficulty in agreeing with Peter
that Paul wrote some things hard to be understood.

Among them we naturally think of his teaching on such subjects as predestination, election,
second coming, women and marriage. But if we
could understand everything in the Bible we
would know that it is human. But because there
are things in the Bible and particularly in
Paul's writings which are hard to understand
we know that they had an origin in a source
which is above our mentality and power to conceive, yea, even divine. And yet I know that
these things were written for our learning and
comfort and that whatever is necessary for our
good will be disclosed by the help of the Holy
Ghost at the time when it is needed. I discover
something new in the Bible every day, something which I never understood before. And I
expect to be continuously finding new things in
the Bible as long as I live.

God gives the understanding of divine revelation only when and where and to whom it is
needed. He gives physical food in the same
manner. He gives oil-producing foods to the
people in the far north because that is what
they need in that climate. He gives citrus fruits
to the southern climates because they are
needed there. And God will give to us an understanding of what we need of His Holy Word
when we need it.

So there are some things hard to be understood, said Peter. Yes, hard to be understood.

There is the doctrine of election. Do you understand all about that? Everytime I preach on election some of my members have spiritual indigestion. They can't masticate it, they can't assimilate it.

Then take, for example, the doctrine of grace. The wonderful doctrine of grace is taught especially in the epistles of Paul. This is hard for some to understand because it runs across their pride and personal ambition. When you are studying the Scriptures always ask the questions, who, when, where, what, why. Here is another important matter and that is to ask, not only who the author is, where it was written, for what purpose it was written, but to ask also to whom is this message addressed? Was it addressed to saints or sinners? Was the address to the church or the world? To Jews or Gentiles?

Another important question to ask is, was the message temporary or permanent? Many people have difficulty with the Bible because they do not distinguish between these things.

Let us take one simple illustration. Here in the Epistle of John it says: ''If we confess our sins He is faithful and just to forgive us our sins and to cleanse us from all unrighteousness.'' That verse has been used by some to lead sinners to Salvation. The sinners are told if they will confess their sins God will forgive them, when that is not true. Now, that verse was not addressed to sinners at all, it was addressed to Christians and it is the Christian who is to confess his sin, with the assurance of forgiveness. This verse is not dealing with the promise of salvation or the way of salvation at all. The sinner receives salvation not by confessing his sin but by accepting Christ as his sin bearer, by accepting Christ as a personal Saviour, who paid the penalty of his sin.

A sinner has no disposition to confess his sin before he is saved. If one could be saved by confession then every thief, and robber and murderer would walk out of prison and go stark free. That is not even sensible — much less good Bible interpretation. This is where we make great mistakes and fall into serious error, by taking the Scripture that was meant to apply to one group and applying it to another group.

It is important to find out what is temporary and what is permanent, in order to properly understand, interpret and apply the Scriptures. Mr. Ramond mentioned the tithe a moment ago, when asking for the evening offering. Now, some say that the tithe does not belong to the new covenant of grace today but that it was a part of the ancient Jewish law. There were two kinds of old Jewish law, the ceremonial law which was temporary and for the Jews only and the moral law, given not alone for the Jews but for all people and therefore permanent. Now, the tithe belongs to the moral law and is therefore permanent, and for all people. The tithe being a part of the moral law is just as binding upon the Christian today as formerly upon the Jew. The moral law says: "Thou shalt not kill, thou shalt not steal." Are we Christians under no obligation to keep these commandments. Yes. Why? Because they belong to the moral law and are permanent. The tithe belongs to the same class.

I fear that the reason why we find so many things in the Bible so hard to understand is due to the fact that we do not want to do what the Bible commands. It is more difficult to obey the Bible injunctions than to understand them. Nothing is quite so hard to understand as that which we do not want to understand.

So, if we are willing to be taught and willing to do what the Bible tells us we may know of the Scriptures whether they be for us or for some one else, whether they apply to our day or some other, whether they be of God or of man.

The second thing which Peter brings out here is that the unstable and the unlearned, wrest Scriptures to their own destruction. The Greek word here translated "unstable" is *astereketos*. It means unsteadfast, mercurial, watery, unreliable, undependable, wishy-washy. Peter may have been recalling his own personal character as it was before he came to Christ. Then he was mercurial. But Christ had made a rock of him. Then he could not understand or interpret the Scriptures. Now it is different. He is now warning the Christians against being led astray by the Gnostic heretics who like his former self are now unstable, unreliable and unsteadfast. They wrest the Scriptures to the destruction of themselves and others. From such may God Almighty deliver us.

They are not only unstable, but unlearned.
And they are not only unlearned, they are non-
learners, they do not study the Word of God.
There are some people who boast of being
agnostics. Agnostic means know nothing. There
was once an agnostic or know nothing political
party in this country. I would not belong to any
group political or religious, which calls itself
agnostic, know nothing. The corresponding
Latin word is ignoramus. An agnostic is an
ignoramus, a know nothing.

These unstable, unlearned people about whom
Peter was writing called themselves gnostics,
Know-it-alls. But Peter said they were agnostics, know nothings. And what is worse they
would not try to learn anything. Ignorance is
tragedy. Wilful ignorance is crime. If knowledge is power, ignorance is weakness. Ignorance may be pitied but cannot be commended
on any ground. Wilful ignorance should be condemned on every ground. Peter, previously
spoke of those who were unable to stop sinning.
Here he speaks of those who are unable to start
learning.

"My people," said the prophet, of the long
ago, speaking for God, "My people perish for
the want of knowledge." And, Jesus said to
the people of His time, "Ye do err not knowing
the Scriptures." Your mistakes and errors and
failures in life are due largely to the fact that
you do not know.

In the third place: They not only are unstable and unlearned, but they actually wrest

and twist the Scriptures into meaning something that they were never intended to teach. Paul refers to this sort of thing in II Tim. 2:15. Hymenaeus and Philetus were among those who erred by misconstruing, misinterpreting and misapplying the Scriptures on the subject of the resurrection and by so doing overthrew the faith of others.

Others have done the same thing with other great doctrines of the Bible, such as the Second coming of Christ, and the Person and Work of the Holy Spirit. These are two favorite subjects for all sorts of vagaries.

The Second Coming of Christ is interpreted to mean that we should lay down everything and go out in the mountains in white robes to look for Christ's return. The work of the Holy Spirit is taken to mean that nothing one does is sin. The doctrine of election is used to mean that some are chosen to damnation and nothing can change it. The doctrine of grace is taught to justify continuance in sin. The Bible teaching on marriage is used as justification for celibacy. And the statements about women speaking in the churches mean they should keep quiet everywhere. And on and on we might go showing how the Scriptures are wrested, twisted, turned around by the unstable and unlearned.

Many come to the Scriptures to find confirmation for their personal opinions instead of information and instruction on their personal conduct. They have some preconceived idea and want a Scripture to back it up. Strangely enough one can always be found, provided it is taken out of its setting.

There is a vast difference between that attitude and a proper approach to the Scriptures, which is to discover what they really teach for faith and conduct.

The deductive method of Bible study is by far the richer and more profitable.

Searching the Scriptures for confirmation rather than for information and instruction has been the cause of divisions and denominations in Christendom.

Yes, our brother Paul said some things hard to be understood. But if we will study them earnestly and prayerfully the Holy Spirit will help us to understand all that we need to know for our best spiritual interests.

1 John 3:16

# 1 John 3:16

CONTINUING our studies in the 3:16's of the New Testament we come to 3:16 of the First Epistle of John, "Hereby perceive we the love of God, because He laid down His life for us; and we ought to lay down our lives for the brethren." May I give you a rather free translation of the text.

By this token we discover the love of God and we have it as a continuous experience because He laid down His life for us. And, if we are Christians we will lay down our lives for the brethren.

Last Sunday morning we had the 3:16 of John's gospel. This morning we have the 3:16 of John's First Epistle.

John's gospel was written to teach lost people how to be saved. John's epistle was written to teach saved people how they may know that they are saved. Now the very heart of John's epistle is 3:16. Tying the two together we have, "God so loved the world that He gave His Son, and by this act we are continuously convinced of the love of God," and are thereby persuaded that; "we ought also to lay down our lives for the brethren."

What if we do not love the brethren? We have not life abiding in us. And if we go beyond that and hate the brethren we are murderers and no murderer has any part in the Kingdom of God.

If we love God that meets the requirement of the first four of the ten commandments. If we love each other that meets the requirements of the last six of the ten commandments. Love is the completion, the fulfilling of all law. And laying down our life for one another is the extreme manifestation, the highest and the fullest expression of love.

It is the highest expression of God's love that He laid down His life for us. It is the highest expression of our love that we lay down our life for the brethren.

Giving money, for the benefit of those who are in need, is in some sense, the giving of our self. Money is coined character, it is minted manhood. But it is not enough. We must give love. Giving time for the service of others is giving something of our self. Benjamin Franklin said, "Dost thou love life? then do not squander time for that is the stuff out of which life is made." But that is not enough. We must give love. Giving faith to either God or man is the giving of some of our self. But it is not enough. Paul speaks of faith that worketh by love. James said that a faith which does not work is a dead faith and useless to both God and man. We must give love.

Sacrificing, even to the giving of every drop of blood in our body, to the giving up of something more precious than life is not enough, we must give love.

To be sure, Christ commands us to take up our cross and to bear it in the interest of others.

Toyohiko Kagawa, now on a speaking tour of
the country, commenting upon this statement of
Jesus, said: "The cross must be overpassed by
love." He found himself criticized by some extreme literalists and legalists in this country.
I have received criticisms of myself from all
over the country for association with and com-
mendation of Kagawa. So I searched out
the quotation in his book "Love the Law of
Life." He says, "The only way of salvation
that I know is that of love. The cross must be
overpassed by love." Well, now any one can
take a sentence out of its setting and criticize it
as an untruth by making it apply to what the
author did not say. This is what the critics of
Kagawa have done. But Kagawa was not speaking of the cross on which Christ died. He was
not discussing the atonement here. He was
speaking of the cross which Christ commands
us to carry in the interest of others. And he
was saying that is not enough, that the cross of
self sacrifice must be overpassed by love.

It is not enough to cast a coin to a beggar on
the street corner. It is not enough to give our
life in sacrificial service for humanity. We must
love that beggar and love that leper and love
that moral derelict and love that criminal in
the name of Christ if we are to win them for
God, and honor Him for "Greater love hath no
man than this that he lay down his life for his
friend."

If you ever drive through Hammond, Louis-
iana, I wish you would pause and view a simple

marble shaft which stands beside the railroad
where you cross it. You will read on it the story
of how James Stewart, a carpenter, cast himself
before an on-rushing train, saved the life of a
little child and lost his own. The grateful family and friends of that little girl erected this
monument to his memory. It is inscribed:
"Greater love hath no man than this that he
lay down his life for his friend." "I am the
good shepherd," said Jesus, "and the good
shepherd giveth his life for his sheep." That
is the highest expression of divine love and of
human love. Not the gift of money, time, talent,
but in lovingly giving one's self for the service
of humanity and for the worship of God — this
is the highest expression of love.

Now what is this love? We talk about love so
glibly that the word rolls off our lips like oil
dripping with distilled sweetness down the
beard of Aaron. But do we know really what it
is?—We speak of baby love, puppy love, physical love, mental love, moral love, family love,
national love, racial love, all these and yet we
do not know what love is. What is love?

Love is described, defined, exemplified by
Christ and recorded in the Bible, as at-one-ness.
I never saw that until I was poring over this
text in the Greek, in preparation of this sermon.
I never had found the real beauty of love until
then. I made a great discovery. Love is at-one-
ness. It is to be at one with another or others.
This word atonement is used only one time in
the New Testament and it means, at-one-ness.

There is real love between brother and brother
when they are one in their common experience
of birth, in their outlook on life, in their purpose and motive in life, in their destiny in life.
When they are at-one-ness there is love. There
is love when husband and wife are at-one-ness.
Their spirits are melted into one. For this purpose shall a man or woman leave father and
mother and cleave to each other. Unless this is
done there is no love, no at-one-ness. You know
how it is, there is disagreement, there is bitterness, there is misunderstanding, there is confusion, love is gone out. When there is at-one-
ness and the two are molded into the crucible of
the fire of self sacrifice into one, that is love,
love divine, all love excelling.

Oh, how wonderful is that love! When God
came down to earth in the person of Jesus
Christ and became a man thus identifying Himself with humanity, becoming one with its sins
and suffering, He gave the supreme token of
His love. Then, I, a man, was given the privilege of rising up to become godlike in Christ.
Christ the Son of God became the Son of man
that the son of man might become the son of
God. The work of reconciliation on the cross
brought God and man into an at-one-ness and
thereby perfected love from and for each other.

God accepted the life of man in Christ that
man might accept the life of God, and the two
thus became one. Now, the basis of real love is
not family, or nation, or race, or education, or
economics, or politics. The basis of real love is

common spiritual experience in which the souls are molded into at-one-ness. God loves, Christ loves, we love and we all become one. God's will becomes our will and God's plan becomes our plan. And because God loves other men and loves us too, therefore, we love each other. The triangle is complete. God loves you and you love God. You are at one. God loves me and I love God. We are at one. Then you love me and I love you. That completes the triangle. The unity is complete and sacrifice and service become an easy thing.

The religion of Christ is not a religion of science, nor of intellect nor of philosophy. It is a religion of love. And love serves. The Bible words which best describe it are bear, share, care. "Bear ye one another's burdens and so fulfill the law of Christ." Do not increase one another's burdens. Many, judged by their conduct, seem to read this: "Multiply one another's burdens." Their sole purpose, in the world, is apparently to make trouble for others, in so doing they fulfil the law of the jungle. "Bear ye one another's burdens," is Christian. Add to one another's burdens is heathenism. Bear ye one another's burdens is Christ-like. Increase ye one another's burdens is devil-like.

Christ's law of love, of atonement, of at-one-ness is: If you have two cloaks and your brother has none, give him one. It is more blessed to give than to receive. Give because you have or else you will be forced to accept because you have not.

All the ills of human society could be cured by this law of love in Christ. If all men were motivated and controlled by love, by a desire to bear, to share, to care, instead of by the desire to get, to have, to keep, then strife, and confusion and wars would end. Those who grasp and get and hold on to things while others suffer want, create bitterness, and hatred and revolution and war.

Sharing with one another, becoming one in suffering and in service, is a great Christian principle. But this sharing must be motivated by love and volunteered, and not forced by law, else it ceases to be Christian.

This principle is set out in Ephesians 4:28:

"Let him that stole steal no more: but rather let him labour, working with his hands the thing which is good, that he may have to give to him that needeth."

We have an illustration of this here in one of our Church Missions. One of our workers over there came to me the other day and told about a family who had been on relief. They came to the mission asking for help, and got it, of course. But the worker told them that they ought to be giving instead of receiving, that they should go to work and earn something to give to others. They were led to Christ. At once life's motivation and purpose changed. They went to work, not to get something for themselves but to get something to give to others. And they have brought an envelope offering to the church every Sunday. Work for what? That you may have something to give to those who have not. Make money for what? For self gratification or for human service?

And right there in that verse I discovered something. And I tell you, there is a thrill, intellectual and spiritual, when you make a new discovery of truth in the Word of God. What is it we find taught in this verse? Here it is, as I see it. Listen: "Labor that you may have, wherewith to help others." That principle put into practice will solve all the problems of labor, of industry and of business. Here is the seed thought for a new, Christianized economic order. Labor, not for yourself in order that you may get more clothes and bigger automobiles, and bigger houses all for yourself. But work that you may have something to give to others. There are millions of people out of work today because they have had nothing but a selfish conception of life and they will continue to be out of employment. Ninety percent of those on relief have no connection with any moral, educational or religious institution or enterprise. Work that you may have something to give to others — that is the proper motive, the Christian motive for getting a job and for making money.

Take a simple illustration. Here are two families living next door to each other. Their family income is $3,000.00 per year. They own their own home. They live comfortably. They each have a small car. Each family is getting along nicely on that $3,000.00. But, naturally they would not be adverse to an increased income. In fact, they rather desire it and would cherish an increase.

Now the income of each family is by some stroke of good fortune suddenly increased to double what they were getting, namely to $6,000.00 per year.

The question is, what was the motive behind the desire for an increase and what did each one do with his increase.

One family purchased a larger house, bought a larger automobile and began living on a larger scale. They became the envy of their neighbors. The hated of the unemployed.

The other family went on living just as they had lived previously within the $3,000.00 limit. They were comfortable, they were happy. Why should they change just to gratify the pride of life and the whims of the flesh?

They sat down and made out a budget for the spending of the additional $3,000.00. They would provide three $100.00 scholarships in a Christian College for worthy students who otherwise could not go to college. They would take care of two children in the Orphans' Home at $150.00 each. They would pay the expenses of a bed in the denominational hospital at $300.00 per year. They would underwrite the salary of a Home Missionary at $1,200.00 and would pay the salary of a Foreign Missionary at $800.00. That would leave them $100.00 for miscellaneous opportunities.

This family, too, became the envy of their neighbors and their example. The poor, the unemployed, all people loved them, admired them and prayed for them.

Which family, think you, did the will of God? Which family got the most out of their extra money?

And there is another thing revealed in this principle. It strikes at one of the crucial points of our capitalistic system in economics and changes the motive for money making from personal profit to social service. It thereby changes the whole order of society from a greedy, selfish gouging of humanity to a loving, helpful brotherhood building up each other, instead of destroying each other.

That Law of love in God changes the whole motive of business from a profit seeking to a service seeking basis. And if it were universally adopted we would see the social order for which poets and prophets and preachers have prayed and hoped through the centuries.

But the godless, selfish profit making for personal gain drives men into all sorts of business. The love of money becomes the root of all kinds of evil! For it men sell liquor, sell character, honor, decency. For it they sell women's virtue and do a thousand other devilish things. If the motive were love and self sacrifice and service, how different would humanity be! There is nothing so beautiful, nothing so dignifying, nothing so glorifying, nothing so satisfying as love motivating our service for others. Love

casts out all fear of each other. Love binds
human society together and all races and peoples become one in the crucible of love where
they are melted into an at-one-ness, into real
love.

During the Japanese-Russian War, Col.
Saito, of the Japanese Army, was sent over to
destroy a bridge of the Russian Army. While
doing so he was captured. He was tried and
condemned to be shot. The Russians said to
him, "What is your last request?"

"My last request is this. Take this bag of
money, one thousand yen, and apply it to the
Red Cross work for the Russian soldiers."

"Don't you mean for the Japanese soldiers?"

"No, I mean to use it for the service of the
Russian soldiers."

And the Russian officer said as he took his
hand and received the gift, "If that sort of
spirit were in the heart of all of us, there would
be no wars."

Love breaks down the barriers and builds up
a brotherhood. As a force from without and
within love overcomes all enemies for love is
supreme.

I was reading a book of science the other day
and I came across this arresting sentence which
captured my thought for a moment. "No bacillus has ever been discovered which can survive
the sunlight." As I pondered that statement
and transferred it from material things to the
spiritual realm I said it is true there, also. The
bacillus of sin, jealousy, pride, hatred, can not

survive the sunlight of God's love, which He
plants in the human heart. The bacilli of all
evils would flee to the dark corners of the earth
if the sunlight of God's love were lighted upon
the altar of all hearts. If your heart is darkened
with selfishness and sin just expose yourself a
while to the love of Christ and let your spirit
catch the glow of a new love, a new life, which
is life indeed. "How dwelleth the love of God
in you if seeing your brother in need you show
no concern for his helpless estate?"

I have been reading a book on ants. They are
very interesting little creatures. They can teach
us much. When a boy I would sit and watch
ants for hours at a time. I learned much from
them. Solomon learned from them and coun-
selled that we go to the ant and consider her
ways. Each ant has two stomachs. One he fills
for his own use. In the other, he carries a surplus of food for his fellow ant, who may be
hungry and without food. That's why they sal-
ute each other when they meet. Finding his
brother in need the ant which has a surplus
gives it to the one who has nothing.

Now that is ant philosophy of life and that is
ant conduct. It is much better than most human
beings have. Go to the ant, thou inhumane human and learn.

We are not only unchristian but we are
actually heathen in our selfishness. We are
worse than the ants. We see our brother in need
and see our fellows in need and do nothing to
help that need.

Love and love alone, conquers all enemies
permanently. No conqueror of the world who
has ever sought to achieve power by force has
ever succeeded permanently. No Czar, Emperor
or Dictator can do it, whether he be political,
religious or economic dictator. From the first
Chinese conqueror through Alexander the
Great, the Caesars, Charlemagne, Napoleon, on
to the Kaiser none has ever succeeded by force.
They all go the way of the world, financial and
economic dictators along with the rest. None
has ever succeeded by force in conquering the
world. They may do so temporarily but like
Napoleon they will die on a lonely island or
like the Kaiser will saw wood in his obscure
Doorn. Force has never accomplished any de-
sired or desirable end. But what force has
failed to do, has been accomplished often by
love. The love of Christ constrains us.

Napoleon asked the question, "What do you
think of Christ?" "What do you think of him?"
was the quick reply. Napoleon said, "Charlemagne and myself built world empires but
upon what did they depend? They depended
upon force. This man Jesus Christ has built
a world empire upon nothing but love. Our
empires have crumbled to the dust and
gone. The empire of Jesus Christ still abides
and there are millions in the earth who would
die for Him at this hour."

Love will produce a paradise on earth. This
is Christianity. The criminal says, "You must
lay down your life for me." The Christian

says, "I lay down my life for you." Now all between these two extremes, the Christian and the criminal, is the balance of humanity.

"This is my commandment," said Jesus, "that ye love one another." Give love and you will have love. Give hatred and you will have hatred. Be lovely and you will be loved.

A child of God should act like a child of God. A prince cannot act like a peasant. A prince of heaven cannot afford to act like a peasant of the earth. Henry Drummond said, "The happiness of love is action. It is a test of what one is willing to do for others." There is the standard by which to measure your Christianity. How much are you willing to do for others? Christ laid down His life for us. We ought also to lay down our life for the brethren.

Revelation 3:16

SO THEN because thou art lukewarm, and neither cold nor hot, I will spue thee out of my mouth.''

That is a terrific phrase to be in the Bible and to be said to a church and to be said by such an exquisitely delightful person as our Lord and Saviour Jesus Christ. This 3:16 is spoken to the last of the seven churches of Asia Minor, to which the Revelation messages were directed. And it is the last word in the last book of the Bible to any church. This is the last time the word church occurs in the Bible for with this ends the church dispensation. God has some other method for dealing with the world following this.

Now these seven churches of Asia to whom these messages were directed have been variously interpreted by expositors and students of the Scriptures.

They have been taken as mere historical churches — the church at Ephesus, the church at Smyrna, the church at Pergamos, the church at Thyatira, the church at Sardis, the church at Philadelphia and the church at Laodicea. They are thought by some as no more than historic churches.

Well, of course that is true, they were historic churches. But there must have been something more to them than that or else the Saviour would not have given such definite, searching messages to these churches. So, looking a little further for the deeper meaning there are those who take it that these churches are typical of churches throughout the ages of Christian history.

Now, if you will read this second and third chapter of the Book of the Revelation and think of your own church, or the church to which you used to belong, or some church that you now know, you will probably find somewhere in these records something that will fit that church about which you are thinking. Thus you will see how these churches of the Revelation message have characteristics which will identify churches of all ages.

There are others who have seen a still further meaning in the messages to these seven churches. That is: that they are intended to represent in the order named, the dispensational dealing of God through the church era of the world. That is to say, each one of these Revelation churches represents a certain period of church history or of Christianity.

' The church at Ephesus represents the period of first expansion and then of declension during the first century, and the second. The church at Smyrna stands for the third and fourth centuries representing the period of persecution and tribulation. The fourth and fifth centuries were the period of Alliances with the forces of the world and are represented by the church at Pergamos. This is the time when the

Roman Catholic church came into existence and
joined up with the government. Then occurred
what we call the union between church and
state which has persisted through the years.
Then came the period of church history from
the sixth through the fifteenth century, the
longest of all the periods, a period of weakness,
of lost spiritual power represented by the
church at Thyatira. And then the Sardis
period of church history, namely the sixteenth
and seventeenth centuries covering the Reformation. During this time those weak, devitalized
and hidden churches began to come forth under
the leadership of Zwingli, and the other great
leaders of the Reformation and burst out into
new life. The eighteenth and the nineteenth
centuries, the period of fraternity, evangelism
and missions, are represented by the church at
Philadelphia. And finally the nineteenth century Apostasy is represented by the Laodicean
church, the church of worldly power and worldly prosperity and of spiritual decay. This was
prophesied and foretold by the condition of the
Laodicean church as a time when from the pul-
pits and Sunday School classes and college
Bible Departments and theological seminaries
and universities, there would go forth all sorts
of false teachings such as denying the deity of
our Lord and Saviour Jesus Christ, or saying
that Jesus never knew He was the Son of God
until He was baptized. Now, of course, there
is something in each one of these churches that
fits the particular period. It does make a re-

markable parallel to place these churches along-
side church history and it certainly furnishes
food for thought and study. It does look as
though God were trying to speak to all the ages
through these church messages. At any rate
this is an ingenious interpretation and is more
easily accepted and understood after the periods are passed than either before or during
the particular period.  '

There were other churches which were more
important historically and otherwise than these
churches of Asia Minor. There was the mother
church in Jerusalem, the missionary church at
Antioch, the Empire church in Rome.

But there must have been, and undoubtedly
was, something, more than the historic value of
these churches which called forth these messages of Jesus to them. With all the regal
splendor and supernal glory described in chapter one, Christ came walking among these
churches with a particular word for each. He
commends some of them, he condemns some of
them, he warns them, he encourages them, he
praises them, he makes promises to them.

Christ loved the church, He died for the
church. Christ has called the church His bride.
It is His field, His force, His temple, His body,
His bride. Christ loved the church and gave
Himself for it, therefore He has a right to criti-
cize it when anything is wrong.

No one has a right to criticize who does not
love and pray for the object of the criticism
and he has no right to criticize unless he is

motivated by a sincere desire of doing good. When criticism is offered one should ask, "Does it come from friend or foe?" If it is from a friend then thank God for it, accept the criticism, profit by it and improve the way whether as individual or church. If the criticism comes from a foe disregard it, treat it with silent contempt. Fault finding is the fun of fools and their folly. But the criticism of a friend who loves with a view of helping is good and should be appreciated. "The rebuke of a friend is better than the kiss of an enemy." I had rather taste the sweetness of rebuke from one who loves than to have the bitterness of a kiss from a hypocrite, a Judas.

No church is perfect, no individual is perfect, no family is perfect because they are made out of imperfect material. Jesus saw the imperfection of these churches and he spoke words of warning and of encouragement in order to strengthen the weak places.

These messages of Christ to the churches are so full of rich material that they have called forth from Alexander Maclaren sixteen sermons from these two chapters alone, and from Sir William Ramsey, the great Archeologist, a vast volume of 450 pages.

Christ reveals to these churches the fact that they are not what they appear to others nor what they think themselves to be, but what they actually are in the white light of his judgment.

One had a name to live but was dead. One thought it was rich and needed nothing, not knowing until Jesus turned on the light that it was poor and naked and miserable and blind.

Jesus knows all about each and every church as He knows the life of each and every individual. He rejoices over the good which He finds and commends it. He sorrows over the bad which He finds and condemns it.

So, when Jesus looked upon these churches He saw that Ephesus needed a revival; that Smyrna needed courage; that Pergamos needed correct doctrine; that Thyatira needed discipline; that Sardis needed spiritual vitality; that Philadelphia needed to see and seize her opportunity for service; and that Laodicea needed to be aroused and awakened.

Thus He calls upon the church at Ephesus to repent; upon Smyrna to endure suffering and to be not afraid, but be faithful to the end; upon Pergamos to purge herself of the Balaamites and Nicolaitans and upon Thyatira to hold fast that which she had and not let it loose; upon Sardis to watch and strengthen her weak places and to guard against the attacks of satan; and upon Philadelphia to hold fast her brotherly love; and to Laodicea, the last church, He makes a declaration and an appeal to be zealous.

In each and every church except Smyrna He finds something to condemn, namely, the backsliding of Ephesus; the false teachers and teaching of Pergamos; the jezebel of Thyatira; the imperfect words of Sardis; the weakness of Philadelphia; and the lukewarmness of Laodicea.

In each and every church except Laodicea He finds something to commend, namely: the labor, patience, works, and moral indignation of Ephesus; the hope and love of Smyrna; the loyalty and faith of Pergamos; the charity and service of Thyatira; the undefiled minority of Sardis; the tenacity of Philadelphia.

It was for Laodicea, the lukewarm, the neither cold nor hot, that He reserved His blistering sarcasm, "I will spue thee out of my mouth."

And now having seen the setting of our 3:16 for tonight in the midst of the seven churches, we find, that it is the last word in the last book, to the last church, during the last appearance, of our Lord on the earth.

This last word is a warning against borderline Christians, a condemnation of twilight Christianity and an appeal for churches and Christians alike to be out and out, open and above board, either one thing or the other.

If the group or organization calls itself a church of God then it should be a church filled with the Spirit of God, proclaiming the word of God, doing the work of God dealing with the souls of men.

Many which call themselves churches are doing a little club work here, a bit of social service there and conducting a makeshift educational program yonder. They are neither church nor club, neither church nor school and because they are half one thing and half the other Christ says, "You make me sick at my stomach like lukewarm water and I will spit you out."

While Jesus was on the earth in the flesh He had said: "He that is not with me is against me and he that gathereth not with me scattereth abroad." To be half and half is worse than to be out and out negative.

In these statements Jesus was only catching up the voice of God His Father which sounded forth through the Old Testament: "Choose you this day whom you will serve." Psalm 119:113 is translated by Moffatt, "I hate men who are half and half." A half breed is persona non grata to both races.

This same note resounds throughout the New Testament. "Quit you like men, watch ye, stand fast, be strong."

There is a futility and a fatality in half heartedness against which Christ warns us.

Border line people find their citizenship more difficult and their lives more unsatisfactory than others.

"Come out from among them and be ye separate," saith the Lord.

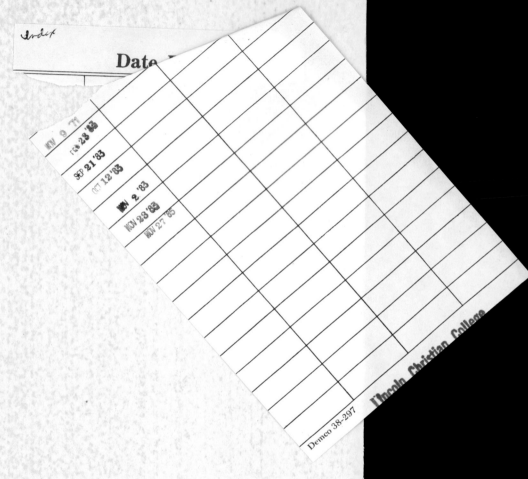